EXPANDING
into LOVE

A Handbook for Awakening to Who You
Are, Raising Your Vibration and
Creating Enlightened Relationships

Diana Rasar, May this book not only expand into love for you but provide you with hope and faith in your future of spiritual growth.

Blessings

Colin [signature]. 3/20/13

COLIN C. TIPPING

Award-Winning Author of *Radical Forgiveness*

Expanding into Love

A Handbook for Awakening to Who You Are, Raising
Your Vibration and Creating Enlightened Relationships

Published in April, 2013
.
ISBN 978-0-9821790-2-4

Global 13 Publications, Inc.
355 Ridge Hill Circle
Marietta, GA 30064

Website: **www.ColinTipping.com**

www.ExpandingInLove.com
(Website for Additional Multi-Media Material)

Cover Design: Andrea Barth and Ian Franklin
Cover Layout: Shari Claire
Proof Reading: Karla Garrett, Shari Claire

Printed in the United States of America.

MORE THAN JUST A BOOK

Technology has changed publishing not only in how books are produced, but in how the content can be linked to websites, photos, videos and audios that support the text and enhance the book. You will find numerous places in the following pages where I suggest watching a video or listening to a particular process in order to get a more rounded and complete experience of the content. While a picture is worth a thousand words, a video adds even more to to the experience.

I have created a special website, *www.expandinginlove.com* exclusive to readers of this book, on which I have posted specific videos, audios or music referenced in the text. I will also add more as time goes on, and update it from time to time as I get feedback and questions from the readers.

If you have a scanner on your mobile device, just scan the QR codes you find on the relevant pages to go direct to the site to see what extra audio/visual content is being offered there, and see or hear it instantly on your smart phone or tablet. This will greatly enhance your 'reading' experience.

In fact, let me invite you to scan it now to go immediately to the website to watch a short welcome message from me on video. It will take you to www.ExpandingInLove.com]
[If you don't yet have a free QR Code scanning app for your smart phone, download one now from your app store.

i

Where the Tools Are

As you already know, or will come to know as you read this book, the power of the Radical Living Strategies lies in using the tools that are associated with each of them. These are listed in Appendix I at the back of this book.

[Many carry no charge and can easily be downloaded by scanning this QR code to go to www.colintipping.com/membership to see them on your smart phone.]

The Radical Living Online Community Resources

Other online tools and processes which tend to be more sophisticated and are experienced interactively over the internet are available there too. However, in order to access these higher level tools and enjoy a whole range of additional benefits, like regular Q&A sessions with me, online study groups and readings based around this book and others, videos and other resources, etc., requires that you become a member of the **Radical Living Online Community.** This is for people who really want to grow spiritually, are committed to embracing the Radical Living lifestyle and wish to be part of a spiritual community that is all about being of service and making a difference.

*[Go to www.colintipping.com/membership, or scan the QR Code to discover the full value of being member of the **Radical Living Online Community**.]*

CONTENTS

INTRODUCTION

T he notion we are exploring in this book is that love leads to expansion while everything unlike love (fear, anger, hate, resentment, control, greed and other such energies) prevents it and leads to a contraction of consciousness. It follows from that, therefore, that we should always choose the path of love in order to expand and do our best to avoid the opposite of it. To do otherwise, surely, would have us remain stuck in a low vibration and failing to grow and evolve.

While it is true that the purpose of this book is to provide the pointers, tools and processes that will help you expand into love, you will find as you read on that the argument it presents will not proceed from the premise stated in the opening paragraph. To take it at face value would sidestep what I believe is essential to our understanding of what love really is, why we are here, how the spiritual world works and how we play our part in it.

The fact is there are times when the path of Love is not always what our soul's growth demands. In the same way that we first need to know darkness in order to experience light, it is necessary for us all to become exposed to the pain of much that is unlike Love in order to learn what Love is and to fully experience Love.

1

Love and Oneness are the same. In order to experience ourselves as Love, we choose during our lifetimes to experience the opposite of Oneness, which is separation. This is why we come to Planet Earth. It is, in fact, our sole purpose for being here.

This is in total contrast with the religious doctrine that says we have fallen from Grace and that God is very angry with us because we experimented with the idea we could be separate, and that we must atone for this 'original sin' if we are to escape God's wrath.

A far more 'Godlike' interpretation of our reason for being here on Earth in a human body is that, far from doing anything 'against' God, we are here to be of service to Him. We have come into this world of form to facilitate the expansion of God Consciousness by providing the opportunity for God to experience itself, through us, as Love—not just as a thought, however, but as a feeling. This is why we each have a body. Without us, God is not.

So, far from committing a terrible sin by becoming human, we have chosen to incarnate so we can achieve this spiritual goal of coming to an expanded awareness of Oneness and thereby evolve to a higher level of consciousness. While we are here on the human plane, pretending to be separate, we experience Love as a deep yearning for connection with everyone and everything—in other words, a profound desire to be who we really are—spiritual beings having a spiritual experience in a human body.

Love is the truth of who and what we are. It is the energy that connects us at the spiritual level. God is Love, we are Love and Love is all there is. Therefore, we do not have to go looking for Love. Love is within us. To expand into it is simply to awaken to the fact that we are nothing but Love.

[Note: It is for this reason that, throughout this book, I capitalize the word 'Love' when used as a noun, Love being the pure expression of the Divine.]

2

This World of Humanity is our school; life is the curriculum, and we get lots of lessons in separation and Oneness every day. Other people, our pets and creatures of the wild are our teachers.

There is every indication, too, that prior to actually incarnating, we engage in some serious discussions with our 'Angels of Incarnation' about how much separation we wish to experience in our upcoming lifetime. Not only do we choose how much of it to have but also what kind of separation we wish to experience. There's plenty to choose from, including abandonment, abuse, exploitation, manipulation, enslavement, discrimination, torture, rejection, betrayal, infidelity, abortion, murder, disease, and so on.

We can also choose to experience the pain of separation from the standpoint of either the victim or the perpetrator. By dividing the world into victims and perpetrators, this ensures we create lots of opportunities to support each other in creating separation. We need both to make it work. Sometimes we are victims, and then at other times we are perpetrators. Either way, it doesn't make any difference because the pain is the same. It's the pain of separation.

However, there does seem to be a need for us to experience it first from one angle, then the other. So, if we have suffered a lot of a particular kind of pain as a victim in a previous life (assuming we believe in reincarnation), we may well select the same thing for this life, but then act it out as the perpetrator this time around. This is known as balancing karma. (What goes around comes around.)

This can occur over and over in our current life also. Karma carries a charge; and for as long as we have it and haven't forgiven the source of it, whether that be oneself or someone else, it will continue to attract or repel anything like itself. We shall see later how this dynamic shows up in all our relationships as a repeating pattern.

The way that the pain of separation is measured is by reference to things called Karmic Units (KU for short). A certain amount of that kind of pain equals one KU, and we choose beforehand, as part of our incarnation contract, how many karmic units to go for.

[Don't worry, KUs are not real, but it helps the narrative to have something that gives a numerical value to the pain of separation.]

Some souls arrange to have a lot of karmic units in their current lifetime while others choose less. It all depends on what we want to learn and what we might have experienced in our previous lives that might need some balancing. It might also depend on how many more KUs we have to garner before we have done enough to know Oneness at the highest level of spiritual awareness, this being, after all, the point of the exercise. The amount of drama you create in your life is an indication of how much spiritual growth you are willing to have in this lifetime. (Isn't this a better way to frame this than calling yourself a drama queen?)

An essential element of this plan is that we forget everything we have agreed upon as soon as we incarnate. We forget all about our life as a spiritual being and have little awareness of the spiritual world we have left. Spiritual amnesia is necessary because we wouldn't feel the pain associated with each separation experience otherwise. We would simply avoid it because we would know it was false and just a game we were playing. We need to be totally unaware of the fact that we have chosen these experiences and are actually co-creating them with other souls for a specific purpose.

There is also a lot of evidence to suggest that a large amount of what happens to us in life is planned prior to our incarnation. It is often the outcome of a number of agreements made with other souls who are incarnating with us. We make contracts with each other to come into our lives at certain times to do specific things that will enable us to experience the pain of separation.

The souls who help us the most are often those we specifically chose to be our parents. If we want to experience a lot of karmic units in this lifetime, who better to get the whole process going than a couple of dysfunctional parents! Early childhood wounds not only give us a lot of karmic units right from the start, but also give us a lot of separation pain to leverage going forward. We leverage the pain and thereby get the most number of karmic units we can out of it by creating a whole series of experiences down the timeline, very much like those we experienced with our parents.

Observing people in our workshops, we discover that a very high proportion of them can indeed identify patterns in their lives whereby they created the same drama over and over with different people as a way to leverage the original pain. If they were abandoned or even just felt abandoned as a child, they find themselves being abandoned in some way by lots of people during their adult lives. Children who were physically or sexually abused typically experience some kind of related abuse throughout their lives, clearly attracting it to themselves. This is highly suggestive that we are creating our life moment by moment as an outplaying of our consciousness and that, furthermore, there is a divine purpose in it.

I used to teach that the purpose for each repetition was to remind ourselves that the original wound remains unhealed and that the purpose of Radical Forgiveness was to heal it. I still do teach it this way to some audiences who might not be ready to look at the Soul's Journey model I am giving you here. Let me show you the logic of this approach on a video and you will see what I mean.

[To watch a video showing this approach in detail, go to www.expandinginlove,com or scan the code.]

But if I remain true to the principle of Radical Forgiveness which says that nothing wrong ever happens, then the word 'healing' doesn't really apply because there's nothing to heal. The original wound was something the soul had chosen, and the parents were carrying out their soul agreement to provide the opportunity. Each repetition thereafter was simply to leverage the pain. So, I took those ideas based on my observations and developed this new hypothetical model to explain how and why we do this journey.

Fig. 1: THE SOUL'S JOURNEY (A Model)

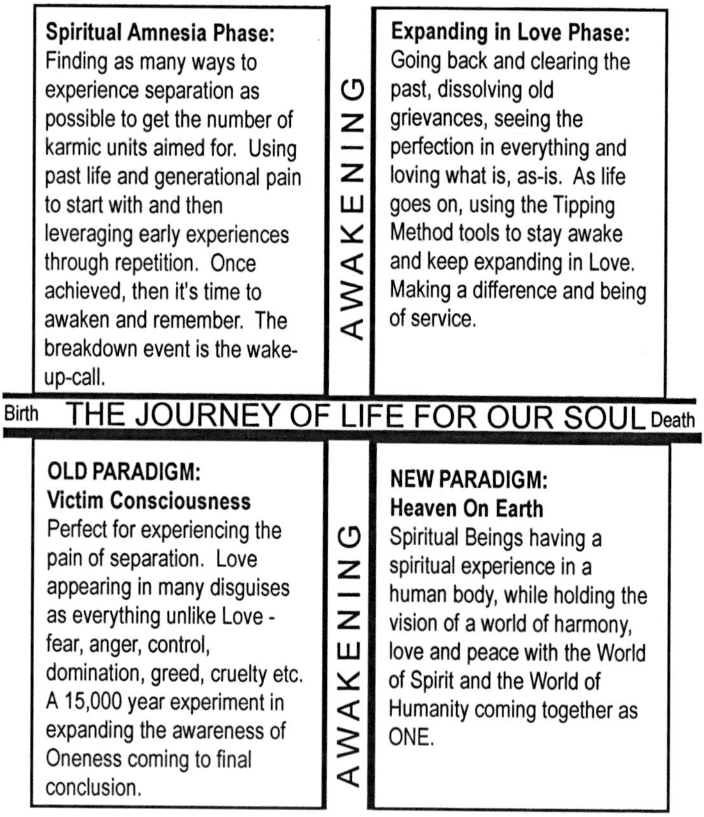

Spiritual Amnesia Phase:
Finding as many ways to experience separation as possible to get the number of karmic units aimed for. Using past life and generational pain to start with and then leveraging early experiences through repetition. Once achieved, then it's time to awaken and remember. The breakdown event is the wake-up-call.

AWAKENING

Expanding in Love Phase:
Going back and clearing the past, dissolving old grievances, seeing the perfection in everything and loving what is, as-is. As life goes on, using the Tipping Method tools to stay awake and keep expanding in Love. Making a difference and being of service.

Birth THE JOURNEY OF LIFE FOR OUR SOUL Death

OLD PARADIGM:
Victim Consciousness
Perfect for experiencing the pain of separation. Love appearing in many disguises as everything unlike Love - fear, anger, control, domination, greed, cruelty etc. A 15,000 year experiment in expanding the awareness of Oneness coming to final conclusion.

AWAKENING

NEW PARADIGM:
Heaven On Earth
Spiritual Beings having a spiritual experience in a human body, while holding the vision of a world of harmony, love and peace with the World of Spirit and the World of Humanity coming together as ONE.

6

[To watch a video explaining this in more detail, go to www.expandinginlove.com or scan the code.]

"Then they got married and lived happily ever after." THE END. This is how fairy tales about relationships usually end and, as a result, give sustenance to the myth that marriage is all about being happy. This myth has given marriage counselors and divorce lawyers, not to mention thousands of authors who have written books and endless magazine articles on the subject, a very good living. All of them try to sell us on the idea that happiness is the purpose of relationship. They are mistaken. The primary purpose of relationships, at least in our unawakened state, is to give us the chance to feel the pain of separation.

Interactions between people, whether within the family or at the workplace, provide endless opportunities to feel separation, and in many different forms: rejection, abandonment, physical abuse, emotional abuse, mental abuse, sexual abuse, rape, incest, lying, betrayal, stealing, infidelity, verbal violence, manipulation, withholding love and support, withholding communication, shaming, down treading, discriminating against, bullying, slandering, etc.

Who else (besides our parents) is better placed to provide such opportunities than our siblings, grandparents, love partners, children, in-laws, co-workers and business partners, not to mention other people with whom we have relationships like religious leaders, doctors, lawyers, police, politicians, and criminals, etc. And don't forget organizations like the government, IRS, churches, the media, etc.

7

This 'Soul's Journey' model is not an easy one to accept, and I do understand why people would say it is crazy. It makes little sense to our rational minds and has very little congruence with what our five senses tell us about the nature of the real world out there.

The only thing I can say in response to that is that when people open up to it, even as just a remote possibility, magic happens. Everything changes. Not only do we feel better – and automatically expand into Love – but everything out there changes too.

So, I invite you to hang in there with me for a while longer to see what might happen for you. There is no need to have belief about it, just the willingness to be open enough to try it. In fact, it is good to have a healthy skepticism about it. I am very skeptical about it myself. But my experience is that it works, so who cares whether it is true or not!

Another thing that makes me think we are all doing this journey for the same reason is that no one seems to get away with it. Rich or poor, we all seem to have some pain of separation show up as part of our (self-created) reality.

Many years ago, my wife and I created an activity called the Radical Forgiveness Circle Ceremony. We have performed this hundreds of times all around the world. Participants stand in a circle, and the facilitator reads out a number of questions. There are usually about 17 of them, asking whether the participants have been victims or perpetrators of some form of 'separation-producing' behavior, such as lying, betrayal, sexual abuse and so on.

If they feel it applies to them, even if it was a long time ago, they are invited to take a silent healing journey by walking across the circle to symbolize their attachment to their victim story and then, after hearing a story that suggests the divine purpose in what happened, walk the circle again expressing their willingness to see the perfection in it.

8

The ceremony is an amazing process in which participants get to forgive themselves and everyone in their whole life; but the point I want to make is no matter where in the world I do the ceremony, and whoever might attend, the response is exactly the same. The 17 questions cover more or less every conceivable form of victimization that exists, and it always happens that people walk the circle for no less than 70-80% of them.

[If you would like to conduct such a Ceremony yourself go to Appendix 1 and find the link for "Ceremony-in-a-Box."]

It seems clear that we are all experiencing the pain of separation, albeit to a greater or lesser degree according to how much we want, and that no one is free from it while they walk this planet. And you have to admit, we all are very good at creating separation. Victim consciousness is still the predominant paradigm that drives the world and has done so for about 15,000 years.

This search for separation does not necessarily continue all through our lives, however. Once our soul is satisfied that it has experienced the amount of separation it needs, we get a message to begin waking up from the dream that, up to now, has been our life. The message is to wake up and remember the truth.

This often happens after a severe bout of separation pain. I call it 'the breakdown experience.' It is often 'the straw that breaks the camel's back,' and forces us to look at our life. That's when we begin to realize that things are not quite as they have always seemed. We slowly become more aware of the fact that life has a spiritual dimension to it and that our lives are indeed divinely guided. We begin to remember who we are: spiritual beings having a spiritual experience in a human body. This is the beginning of our 'awakening.'

[Note: In using the term 'awakening,' I am aware of the potential risk of indulging in spiritual grandiosity. The term is often used to describe the experience of spiritual masters like Buddha and Jesus becoming 'enlightened.' We are using the term 'awakening' here in a more ordinary sense to indicate a rather sudden and sometimes dramatic increase in one's awareness of spiritual reality. For some, it comes as an epiphany, while for others it is experienced as a gradual realization.]

From that moment on, your life begins to change. That's assuming, of course, that you have some years left and that you want to continue the life experience. I suspect that only a few decades ago and for most people, the awakening happened at the moment of death. But now, with a general rising of consciousness, this happens for a lot of people around the mid-life mark. It takes as long as it takes in order to create the amount of separation you signed up for; but as life has speeded up, so have opportunities to experience separation increased.

The people who come to my Radical Forgiveness workshop are usually aged 40 and above. Many of them are in their 60s and 70s. That's not to say they haven't been awake for some time, but they still come to work through all the old baggage of the past.

You, dear reader, must be either just entering the awakening phase or have already begun the awakening process. Otherwise you would not be reading this book. Of that, I am certain.

If you had not yet reached the point of awakening you would not be attracted to the book, or if you were to buy it, you would have put it down. Only when you had reached the point of awakening would you have picked it up again. That's because, up until the point of awakening, you would still have needed to experience everything that was (seemingly) unlike Love as a way to build up your desired number of karmic units.

Your own experiences of separation would have caused you pain, judging them as bad, unfortunate or even tragic. And you would have felt the pain as fear, anger, resentment, jealousy, hurt and so on. But in reality, there was nothing wrong with those things because, as you now know, they had a spiritual purpose. That means they are Love, too, appearing in a whole range of different but incredibly effective disguises.

This is what we mean when we say "Love is All There Is." If everything is there as the means to bring us to a point where we can awaken and then expand into Love, then there is nothing that is not Love. After the awakening, the purpose of life is to become aware of this fact, recognizing in every moment that there is only Love. Love is having the full awareness of the perfection in everything and knowing we are all One. It is the *acceptance* of what is, as is. (Fear is the *resistance* to what is, as is.)

The great paradox for us, then, lies in the fact that we can ONLY expand into Love if we recognize the perfection in everything that we have hitherto considered, in our unawakened state, as being less than Love. It is only when we can be open to the idea that things like fear, anger, pride, cruelty, violence, genocide, and so on, all have a divine purpose in the grand scheme of things that we will be able to expand into Love in any meaningful way.

But in order to do this, we require help. We need a set of signposts, markers and maps to guide us on our journey from the old paradigm to the new one. Once we are there, we need some practical, down-to-earth tools to help us live our lives as awakened human beings while at the same time being able to cope easily with everything at the level of everyday reality.

This is the lifestyle that I call **Radical Living**. It is the kind we need to adopt if we are to remain awake and stay connected to the perfection of what is at all times. After all, it is easy to choose to feel Love when life is really smooth and we are at peace. It is not so easy when we have to deal with the kind of challenges that life continually throws at us, even when we are awake. We still need all the help we can get.

In Chapter 14, we explore how to develop a Radical Living Lifestyle, but part of what it means to begin living it is having the intent to look back at all that has happened to you in life up to this moment and to find the willingness to see the perfection in everything. That is the first step in the process of expanding into Love, and I will explain in later chapters how this can be achieved. Then it will be a case of learning how you can respond to the events which happen to you from this point on, or in the post-awakening phase of your life, by choosing the path of Love as we have newly defined it, not as a rejection of anything unlike Love but as an acceptance of everything just the way it is.

Nowhere is this lesson better learned than in relationship, which is why so much of this book is concerned with how we do that particular dance as part of our soul's journey. Each of the souls we come into relationship with, whether for just a few minutes or for many years, agrees to provide opportunities for each of us to feel the pain of separation in a variety of ways and then, once awakened, to learn how to love in the ways we have just described.

Finally, we can easily look at this model and imagine that what applies to individual human beings like you and me, is every bit as applicable to humanity itself. If we were to construct a timeline for the whole human race stretching way back to the time we first began walking upright, it might look just like our own.

This possibility is explored in much greater depth in Chapter 15, but suffice to say here that for eons humanity has been living the illusion of separation through what we loosely call civilization.

12

And it shows every sign of having reached the 'tipping point, (wish I'd thought of that!) where it would implode in on itself and suffer a complete break down.

That might well be the moment at which we, as a species, having completed our group soul assignment wake up and realize who we are and why we are here. The great experiment with the energy of separation will have come to an end and everyone on the planet will EXPAND INTO LOVE in a way that will give a whole new meaning to this book's title. Stay tuned!

[To watch a video of of me expanding on Humanity's own Soul Journey that might put into context for you what is going on in the world right now and possibly in the near future, scan the QR Code tor go to www.ExpandinginLove.com.]

 [A nice way to bring this Intro to a conclusion is to suggest you listen to a song by Karen Taylor-Good called "Try to Remember." Go to the "Music" section at www.ExpandinginLove.com or scan the QR Code. It makes a great segue into the next chapter.]

PART ONE

LOVE AND RELATIONSHIP

1. Love Is

Of all the millions of songs ever written and performed, and of all the poems, stories and letters which make up the literary legacy of every country in the world, the vast majority have been about love in some form or another. You would think, therefore, that to ask 'What is love?' is a stupid question. Surely we all know what it is. Or do we?

In the Introduction, I defined 'Love' as the willingness to see and feel the Divine Love flowing through everything, no matter what is happening. It is the kind of Love we fall into only when we have awakened and have glimpsed what lies beyond our limited five-sensory reality and have come to understand who we are, why we are here and what we are destined to do with our lives. I will come back to this later to show how we can expand into this kind of Love in our everyday lives once we are awake.

Meanwhile, let's look at some descriptions of the kinds of love that we might be able to recognize and may even have experienced in our own human relationships. The Ancient Greeks had four words to describe the different kinds of love which flow between people, and the distinctions are still useful today even though there is still quite a bit of overlap. The words used to describe the four different kinds of love were Agápe, Eros, Philía, and Storge.

1. Agápe love is described as being a deep and enduring 'true love" in the fullest sense of that word. It is a deep, caring love that exists between two people who have a strong and abiding affection for each other, which continues to exist irrespective of circumstance. The nearest translation of Agápe love is unconditional love; and its source is the Love which flows from God, Spirit, Universe or the All That Is, by any other name. (I use the term 'God' here for convenience.)

However, there has been a tendency to equate Agápe love to unconditional love in the literal sense of it being a form which is 100% free of judgment, expectation or reservation. Furthermore, since there are no conditions attached, it can never be withdrawn or compromised, no matter what happens or how undeserving of love the person seems to be. It's an all-or-nothing idea. You cannot be unconditionally loving in a partial or selective sense.

While this is true of God's Love, which I will come to in a moment, the effect of such a literal interpretation of Agápe love, insofar as it applies to humans, has been to remove this form of Love from the possibility of it ever being experienced or demonstrated by human beings other than the likes of Jesus and Buddha. Given our current state of consciousness, we are totally incapable of unconditional love if we take it so literally. Our love is always conditional, conditioned upon the person who is the object of our affection remaining 'lovable.'] How many people do you know who would say they truly love Hitler, Stalin or the serial killer, Jeffrey Dahmer. A mother's love is probably the nearest we come to unconditional love, but it still remains conditional at heart. I prefer to use the term 'Agápe love' in the way it was originally used, as being such a deep caring for the person that it is worthy of the term 'true love' and regarded as being as near to unconditional as is humanly possible. Perhaps the Buddhists come closest to unconditional love in how they describe Love as being compassion.

Love As Compassion *(The Buddhist definition.)* In its highest form, compassion occurs when, through our ability to empathize with people, we begin to merge with them as if there were no separation. We become one with the other person and feel their pain and their joy as if it were our own. We wish for what they desire as fervently as they do themselves.

When we are able to be totally with someone in their suffering, doing everything in our power to alleviate the pain but not so overwhelmed by it that we are unable to see the hand of God in the situation, that is true compassion. To be able to do so, we need the spiritual power that Radical Forgiveness gives us to hold the vision that Divine Love is everywhere and no one is forgotten

2. Éros is the kind of love that is characterized by sexual attraction and desire. It is a romantic love in which the lover is consumed with passion, sensual desire and longing for an emotional connection with the other. It is also deeply appreciative of the beauty of the inner person as well as the outer physical form. In that sense it should not be considered merely driven by lust. It can lead one in the direction of finding spiritual truth in the love bond which arises in Eros and ultimately in becoming aware of the Love of God flowing through oneself. When that happens, Agápe love and Eros begin to merge.

The following quote by Pope Benedict XVI in his first Encyclical *Deus Caritas Est,* which is Latin for *'God is Love,'* illustrates this joining of these two forms of love, one that ascends and the other that descends with both ultimately becoming unified in the reality of the love of God.

"...eros and Agápe—ascending love and descending love— can never be completely separated. The more the two, in their different aspects, find a proper unity in the one reality of love, the more the true nature of love in general is realized. Even if eros is at first mainly covetous and ascending, a fascination for the great promise of happiness, in drawing near to the other, it is less and less concerned with itself, increasingly seeks the happiness of the other, is concerned more and more with the beloved, bestows itself and wants to "be there for" the other. The element of Agápe thus enters into this love, for otherwise eros is impoverished and even loses its own nature. On the other hand, man cannot live by oblative, descending love alone. He cannot always give, he must also receive. Anyone who wishes to give love must also receive love as a gift."

Co-dependence

This is where love, which may initially seem to have arisen out of genuine physical attraction, reveals itself as a Faustian bargain which is negotiated and struck on the basis of mutual and pathological neediness. Both partners sell their souls in order to feed their respective neuroses.

The narcissist needs a partner who will always put him or her first and willingly subjugate him/herself to the narcissist's happiness. The co-dependent partner on the other hand needs someone upon whom they can lavish attention in order to feel wanted. Clearly then, narcissists and 'people-pleasers' are magnets for each other and together create a neurotic co-dependent relationship.

The co-dependent partner does not say, but will always imply, *"I will always be here for you, take care of you and do everything to ensure your pleasure and comfort, just so long as you tell me every day that you love me and cannot do without me."* To complete the bargain, the narcissist will also imply, without saying, *"I will tell you every day that I love you so long as you fulfill my need for what I unconsciously feel is my right to have."*

So long as this bargain is maintained, the relationship will work; but there will be no Love in it. No matter how it looks on the surface, the co-dependent relationship has a foundation based on dysfunction, denial and an unwillingness to heal the neuroses which created the neediness in the first place. Should one partner break their side of the bargain, then whatever looked like love in the beginning will rapidly turn to hate.

Co-dependent people have what is known as a 'Type C' personality which is characterized by denial of feelings, low self-esteem and an excessive concern for the needs of others to the detriment of themselves. They are the people-pleasers, rescuers and caretakers of this world. [I once heard someone give a humorous definition of a co-dependent as one for whom, when they have a near-death-experience, someone else's life flashes before their eyes.]

In the book, *The Type C Connection*, authors Tamoshek and Dryer show how people who exhibit the Type C personality are far more likely to get cancer than people who do not repress their feelings in this way or subjugate their own needs for the sake of others. In fact, they cite one study by researcher, Stephen Greer, who has proven that this kind of behavior is one of only two actual predictors of cancer, the other one being the genetic factor.

A marriage built on co-dependence might last many years, but there will be little Love in it. There will also be a lot of denial in it too because both spouses will present a good face and even kid themselves that it is working. There will be lots of opportunity to feel the pain of separation in this kind of relationship.

3. "Philia" is the kind of love which exists between family members (not all perhaps), very close friends and even business partners. It exhibits and demands loyalty and commitment to an ongoing deep relationship which cannot be easily broken. It is often expressed as brotherly love. It is the kind of love that soldiers feel for each other when they are in battle, willing to sacrifice and even die for it. For many people who have experienced war, such a bonding is the most intense feeling of love they will ever experience. (By the way, love and liking may not always go together. Two soldiers may dislike each other but might nevertheless be willing to die for each other.)

If the Philia bond is broken, it can be the cause of intense pain and long-term suffering. Lovers can also experience this kind of love, but probably the most intense form of Philia is that which exists between identical twins. This is where we see Philia being as much a soul-to-soul connection as it is a love bond between two human beings.

4. "Storge" is the love or affection which may occur naturally and automatically as between parents and children. It can also develop out of a relationship characterized by a feeling of complete familiarity and, to some extent, may be assumed or taken for granted and naturally conferred when needed. It is this kind of love that strengthens and maintains the family bond and keeps it functioning in spite of everything. Storge is often reinforced with ritual in the home, such as family mealtime get-togethers, religious rituals and celebration of birthdays, anniversaries, weddings and funerals.

Love of one's neighbor as an accepted moral obligation is a form of Storge love that binds a community together and can even extend to people who are personally unknown to us but are included nevertheless, especially when times are hard and neighbors have to depend on neighbors for love and support. In its fullest expression, it is not dissimilar to unconditional love in the sense that it can endure in spite of a great deal of abuse and rejection being returned. We see this when parents continue to love their teenage offspring in spite of the hatred and rebelliousness that some teenagers can express towards their parents.

At the receiving end, there can often be a high expectation attached to this kind of love; and it may even be demanded, especially in families where religious and cultural mores are strictly enforced. Love can be ruthlessly withdrawn if a child chooses to marry someone not approved of by the parents or decides to switch religious affiliation. Consequently, it can lead to a lot of pain and anguish if the expectation is not met.

In my Radical Forgiveness workshop, when we address the issue of our pain and discomfort arising from holding unrealistic expectations, I always ask this question: "What right do you have to demand that your mother love you?" They look at me as if I am crazy. "Well, our parents should love us," they say. "It's only natural." That's Storge.

I am not exaggerating when I say that no matter what the issue people come to work through at my intensive, when we dig deep to find the real wound underneath the presenting problem, in at least 80% of the cases, it comes down to "my mother (or father) didn't love me enough - or not in the way that I needed

23

it to be shown." Another complaint, especially from women is, "My father wasn't there for me emotionally." That's how important Storge is in most people's lives; and as we shall see in the pages ahead, it can affect our whole life.

But can love of any kind be demanded or assumed? If parental love is not there, is the parent to blame? What if our mother or father does not have the capacity to love? Or if he/she does have the capacity, what if he/she can only show it in ways that are not satisfying for us?

At the human level, love is selectively given and is always conditional. While you can be *willing* to love someone, you cannot *will* yourself to love anyone. Love is either there or it is not, and there's not much you can do about it. You can do your best to see the good in people, have compassion for them, and be charitable towards them by accepting them the way they are; but that is not the same thing as Love. You can appreciate them for who and what they are; but again, it is not really the same thing as Love, unless we are using 'love' in the same way as when we say, "I love ice cream," or "I love good food."

Love Creating Separation
During the pre-awakening phase, love and separation are two sides of the same coin. We use love to create our lessons in separation. When we 'fall in love,' we create expectations and attachments to the beloved person as a way to set ourselves up for the pain of disappointment and loss when such expectations are not met and the attachments fail to satisfy.

We also use Love, or what we think of as love to possess, dominate and control the one we love. These limited forms of love will be experienced as separation, and in that sense, will have served their function for the soul's purpose. That's why it is perfect.

24

It draws us in with the promise of wholeness and then creates separation by turning to hate, jealously, domination and control, thus revealing itself as a sham. At that point, we 'fall OUT of love' and then seek to fall IN love with someone else, only to find that nothing has changed.

It will continue in this way until the point is reached where our soul has experienced the amount of the pain of separation it wanted to experience in this lifetime. Only then will we become free to expand into a Love that is real, enduring and authentic, one that features the very best of Agápe, Eros, Philia and Storge love. Only then can we really connect with the Love that is within us all the time. Only when we cease to see separateness in any form and recognize that every human being is an expression of the Divine, can Love become close to being unconditional. Herein, then, lies the ultimate goal of expanding into Love—simply to become Love. And as we become Love, we expand the consciousness of God.

To become Love is a state of being where you are simply a channel for the Divine Love that flows to everyone irrespective of relationship. It is Agápe love in its purest form. It is the kind of love that asks nothing and gives everything. It is a spiritual state of consciousness where you are not loving something or somebody; rather you simply are Love. It is a state of being. Jesus didn't just love; he was Love. His Love demanded nothing in return. When a person is simply Love, it emanates from them, and it is enough to be in their presence.

Since we were created in the image of God and God is Love, then this means we are extensions of His Love. Our true nature is Love, and the purpose of our soul's journey is to expand into it.

Loving Yourself
I cannot leave this chapter without speaking of the need to extend Agápe love to oneself. Many will admit that while they are able to

love others relatively easily, they have a hard time loving themselves. In the spiritual amnesia phase, self-loathing is, of course, simply another way of feeling a very painful form of separation within ourselves. The problem is, however, that it becomes so deeply imbedded in our consciousness that even when we have begun our awakening, we forget to let go of the false perception that we are not OK.

We continue to use destructive self-talk to deny ourselves the compassion, mercy and grace we are willing to extend to others. Even when we have awakened, while we see others as divine beings, we withhold that benediction from ourselves by berating ourselves for being 'not awakened enough,' or 'not spiritual enough' to qualify.

The truth is that we are perfect the way we are, always have been and always will be. Of course, as spiritual beings living a human life, we will appear as less than perfect; but from a spiritual point of view, our perfection lies in our very imperfection. Without our seeming imperfections, the game of life would not function. We are living our destiny exactly as was agreed before our incarnation, which means we are just as worthy of God's Love and, therefore, our own Love, as is anyone else. We are all children of God, and God's grace is with everyone, no matter what they are doing and have done.

That said, I know how difficult it can be to love ourselves in our imperfection. I have listened to a lot of spiritual teachers telling me that I should love myself. But they never told me how. Neither did they ever give me any tools which would push me in the direction of self-love and help me overcome my self-hatred. This is why we have a section on Self-Forgiveness and Self-Acceptance in Part Four of this book.

But here's another way to practice developing love for yourself—love others as enthusiastically as you can. It is often said that you cannot love others if you haven't first found Love for yourself. I disagree. When you focus on giving love to others, it is impossible not to feel good about yourself. It is heart-warming to give Love, and it is your heart which is warmed as well as the heart of the beloved. When you love others, the Love is mirrored back to you immediately and in the same measure. You can't avoid it because if you love someone, your heart is already open. Giving and receiving are the same.

Conversely, if you think you must love yourself before you can love others, you begin the effort with your heart closed. And as you turn inwards to find Love for yourself, you meet up with all the characters that live in your head who feel it is their duty to deny you Love. Your inner critic will tell you everything that is wrong with you. Your inner judge will sentence you to a lifetime of self-hatred. Your inner priest will tell you you're not worthy of Love, least of all the Love of God. No luck there.

So, if you want to develop real Love for yourself, start by seeing the perfection in everyone around you, and let that perfection shine the light on your own unique perfection. Love can only produce Love. Whenever we are loving someone, or some thing, we are always loving ourselves and, by extension, God. If God is perfect and we are 'little bits of God Stuff,' then we too must be perfect.

I have tried hard, without success I have to say, to find out who wrote the following celebration of our individual uniqueness. Whoever wrote it deserves our thanks.

> *YOU ARE SPECIAL. In all the world there is nobody like you. Since the beginning of time, there has never been another person like you. Nobody has your smile. Nobody*

*has your eyes, your nose, your hair, your hands, your voice.
You are special.*

*No one see things just as you do. In all of time there has
been no one who laughs like you, no one who cries like you.
And what makes you laugh and cry will never provoke
identical laughter and tears from anybody else, ever.*

*You are the only one in God's creation with your set of natural
abilities. There will always be somebody who is better at
one of the things you are good at, but no one in the Universe
can reach the quality of your combination of talents, ideas,
natural abilities and spiritual abilities.*

*Like a room full of musical instruments, some may excel
alone, but none can match the symphony sound of the Family
of God when all are played together because God set the
members - every one of them - in exactly the right and perfect
arrangement.*

*Through all of eternity, no one will every look, talk, walk,
think, or do exactly like you. You are special. You are. And,
as in all rarity, there is great value. Because of your great
rare value, you need not attempt to imitate others. You should
accept - celebrate - your differences and even those parts of
yourself that you judge to be not OK.*

*You are special. Continue to realize it's not an accident that
you are who you are. Continue to see that God created you
special for a very special purpose. God called you out and
ordained you to a calling that no one else can do as well as
you. Out of all the billions of applicants, only one qualified,
only one has the best combination of what it takes. That
just as surely as every snow flake that falls has a perfect
design and no two designs are the same, so within the Family*

of God also, no two people are the same, and without each member, the Family would be lacking. God's plan would be incomplete.

Ask God to teach you your Divine Plan for life. Let it unfold in perfect sequence and perfect order in such a way as to bring the greatest glory to God! ***You are celebrated for who you are, just the way you are.***

[If you would like to hear me reading this piece go to www.ExpandingInLove.com or scan this QR code to go there directly. Select the Audio option.]

2. The Purpose of Relationship

The purpose of relationship is two-fold. During the spiritual amnesia phase we come together in relationship in order to provide each other lessons in separation. After the awakening, we come together to help each other Expand into Love. It's that simple.

I will deal first with the idea that the purpose of relationship is to give us experiences that expand our awareness of our separation even while it moves us in the direction of awakening and becoming whole. Then I will cover how, once we have actually awakened, the purpose shifts into how we support each other in staying awake, expanding in Love and living life according to the new way of looking at the world we have woken up to.

Looking first at relationships from the point of view of them giving us opportunities to feel the pain of separation, it is frequently the case that relationships are created through the Law of Karma. I mentioned earlier that our own karma, in the form of residual energies associated with unhealed issues with people such as one or both parents, siblings, abusers, authority figures, etc., will cause us to attract into our lives people who resonate with these residual energies. Later on, perhaps, when we have awakened, they will help us heal that pain. But not yet. We have more karmic units to earn first.

31

So, having found someone who 'resonates' with our karma, whether it be karma from a previous life or from a childhood wound in this life, we first 'fall in love' with the person and then begin to use the relationship to leverage the original pain that gave rise to our karma. That way, we get more karmic units out of the original pain that sourced the karma in the first place.

[It might be helpful here to look at a brief recap of the Soul's Journey, just to remind yourself of how we keep on creating the same kind of pain of separation until we have garnered the number of karmic units we signed up for. Go to www.expandinginlove.com, or scan the QR code.]

How Have YOU Leveraged Your Karma?

It might be interesting to take a look at some of your early childhood wounds or unresolved issues and how you have leveraged that pain by recreating it many times over during your adult life. Take a moment to see how you have done that in your own relationships by taking this brief quiz. First, review your romantic relationships from an early age to now and then **answer yes or no to the following questions.**

a) Have your relationships all lasted approximately the same length of time before declining or even ending? **YES/NO**

b) Do you have difficulty sustaining a long-term relationship? **YES/NO**

c) Is your spouse like your parent of the same sex, at least in some respects? **YES/NO**

d) Do you have a tendency to attract the same kind of person to be in relationship with each time? **YES/NO**

e) Do your partners seem to be wonderful for the first 6 months or so and then turn abusive? **YES/NO**

f) Do you always end up getting hurt? **YES/NO**

g) Are you unable to attract a partner? **YES/NO**

If you answered 'Yes' to any of these questions, there is some kind of underlying energetic pattern you are using to leverage the original pain in order to get more 'Karmic Units' out of it. Let's look at each one in detail.

[Don't worry. God has his own computer to keep the accounting of Karmic Units right. When you have experienced enough separation to have earned the number of karmic units you signed up for, God lets you know.]

The Results

If you answered 'Yes' to (a) and/or (b), then it is likely that you experienced a trauma at the same age as the length of time a relationship typically lasts. This created in you a belief that *"good things can only last this length of time, and then they go bad."*

For example, suppose your father left home when you were five. Everything was fine up to that point in your life. You felt loved by him, and you were secure in that love. When he left, you were devastated and your whole life changed. That was painful, of course. But then you leveraged that original pain by perhaps a factor of ten by adopting a whole string of false ideas and erroneous beliefs, such as:

"All good things only last five years."
"All men will leave me after five years."
"I don't deserve to have happiness in relationship for more than five years."
"If I allow myself to love, I will be hurt. It is best that I close my heart and avoid relationships altogether."

[To watch a video with me showing this process in a more dynamic way than I can just by writing it, go to www.expandinginlove.com or scan the QR code to go directly to it.]

These beliefs became self-fulfilling prophecies in your adult life and may well still be creating your life to this day, or did until you awakened and decided to trash them. By living your life out of such beliefs, and creating a series of relationships that proved you right about your beliefs, you have elevated that original pain into a lifetime of suffering, limitation and loneliness. That has given you a load of karmic units. Merely through leveraging one or two events like this, you may well have reached your goal earlier in life than you otherwise would have, had you only kept to creating a lot of small, painful events. But you couldn't have done it without being in relationship with people who would play your game.

A very common wound suffered by young children, which is often leveraged, is the death of a grandparent. It is usually their first experience of death; and since the bond between grandparent and grandchild is often very strong, that experience is usually traumatic and the sense of loss profound. The child may not understand why the object of their affection and the source of their own self-worth has suddenly gone away. He/she may even assume some blame for the death, or feel they could have done something to prevent it.

Parents unwittingly compound the wound by shielding children from the reality of the death by not allowing them to see the body or be part of the grieving process. They try to cover it over and tell the child, "Don't cry. Granddad is in heaven now," or offer some other (for a young child at least) equally meaningless story and perverse version of reality, which I am sure the child seldom ever buys. By not allowing the child to express his/her grief at this most critical event, the parent infers that emotions are bad and should not be felt or expressed. The child then makes a decision: "Better that I shut down my capacity to feel anything in the future." This sets the child up for a lifetime of being disconnected from his/her feelings and, at worst, bereft of the capacity to love or form strong relationships, fearing the 'other' might die or disappear.

If you answered 'Yes' to (c) and/or by extension, (d), you almost certainly have unresolved issues with that particular parent or the other. The most common example is where a woman who had an alcoholic father marries a man who is also an alcoholic or becomes one very soon after. If a woman had an abusive father, she is almost certain to attract a man who will abuse her as well. A man whose mother exhibited weakness and neediness, for which he judged her severely, will likely marry a girl who is also dependent on him for supplying her emotional needs. And so on. I see this all the time in my workshops, so I know it to be very common.

If you answered 'Yes' to (e), it comes as a consequence of our developing the kind of intimacy *(into-me-see)* in which the masks we usually wear at the beginning of a relationship begin to slip. What is then revealed in the other person is some ugly shadow material that was completely hidden up to that point. Whereas you had always seen this person up to now as (say) a loving and caring person, you suddenly discover a nasty cruel streak underneath that veneer which starts showing up after about 6 months. So you run away. This is why your relationships tend to last only a short while. This dynamic is, in fact, an opportunity to feel the separation within yourself, because what this person is doing is reflecting back to you the parts of yourself that you have denied and repressed. We will come back to this in PART FOUR when we look at how dynamics like this can bring us back to a wholeness and an expanded Love for ourselves. Prior to the awakening, however, we just use it as another way to experience the pain of separation.

If you answered 'Yes' to (f), then it is likely that you have a belief deeply imbedded in your consciousness that you deserve to be treated badly or hurt in some way. This can be connected to how you were treated as a child, always feeling unsafe perhaps, or abused in a way that made you feel you weren't worthy of receiving love and caring, or in some way didn't deserve to be treated with care and respect. Plenty of karmic units in this situation.

If you answered 'Yes' to (g), then because of how you were treated at home as a child, you developed a belief that you don't deserve to have a relationship, or are not worthy of one, or that you are not lovable. (Note: If you want a relationship, Chapter 16 provides the key to creating one.)

I will show you later how all these issues can be resolved easily and quickly using the tools that The Tipping Method provides. For now, though, we simply need to see these things as the perfect way to leverage the pain of separation. We might also need to remind ourselves that the original karma we used as leverage, like the childhood wound, was also self-created and chosen by our soul.

Now look to see if any of the following have repeatedly shown up in most, if not all, your relationships?

> Betrayal
> Abandonment
> Severe Disrespect
> Being Discounted and Ignored
> Lies and Withholding of Information
> Deceit and Secrets
> Infidelity
> Control and Manipulation
> Physical Abuse
> Emotional and Mental Abuse
> Sexual Abuse

Severe Rejection
Punishment
Other

If so, it is a reflection of a core-negative belief that you deserve to be treated in this way. Someone planted that idea in your mind at some time, so you could use it to garner more karmic units through the leveraging principle. Again, in Chapter 19, I will show you how to dissolve all these beliefs, so make a note of which ones have been part of your consciousness, up to now or during the amnesia phase.

Pain in the Bank
Another great source of emotional pain, based on many different forms of separation, is available to us from what was handed down from our family of origin and our ancestors. It is known as generational karma. While it is true that in our own generation, we are somewhat willing to talk about our feelings, our forefathers were masters of suppression and repression of their pain. So they stored it up. But it did not go away. It got handed on down to the next generation, on to the next and so on down the line.

Some say we are all dealing in some way or another with the unresolved pain of our ancestors up to seven generations back. Scientists have shown very recently that emotional pain actually gets handed down through the genes via the epi-genome.

In my own workshops, what I get to see most is people acting out the pain of their mother and less frequently, their father, or one of their grandparents. They don't realize it, of course, because they have made the pain their own; but to a trained observer, it is obvious.

But besides the generational pain that comes from our own family, we are also carrying generational pain derived from the collective experience of large groups of people to whom we are connected. This is known as group karma.

Persecuted religious groups to which you might have connections would be one example. A gay person would, even in today's more liberal environment, be carrying the pain of those who in an earlier time were shunned, vilified and even outlawed. Blacks still have a great deal of anger that comes from slavery, while white people still feel the shame for having perpetrated it. This is heavy karma which many people are still carrying and using to garner karmic units.

Exercise
It will be worth taking a moment to look at some of the issues that cause you pain and anguish, even after you have awakened, and to assess whether or not that pain has been handed down to you. More importantly, you should ask yourself whether you are entitled to make that pain your own? If not, give it back and let it go. Don't hand it on to your children. Let that buck stop here!

1 Type of Pain: *(Guilt, Shame, Anger, Fear etc.)*

_____

2. Carried For: *(Parents, Grandparents, Siblings, etc)*

_____

3. Taken On When? *(Age and/or Event)* _____

4. Played Out How? *(Self-Sabotage, Blaming, Sickness, Bad Relationships, Poverty, Loneliness, Failure, etc.)*

_____

Now Read Out Loud: *"I now realize that this pain is not my own and I am not entitled to it. I took it on in order to help but in keeping it I have robbed _____ of the gift the pain brings. I release the pain now and forever."*

It is little wonder then that our souls use marriage and, more recently in our society, serial marriages and blended families, same sex marriages and many forms of committed relationships that are not marriages, as a way to experience the pain of separation. It provides a wellspring of opportunity for a soul seeking such experiences. Even a relationship that arises out of genuine romantic love will begin to degenerate into a subtle and sometimes not-so-subtle political game in which one seeks to dominate, exploit, control and manipulate the other person in order to satisfy one's own needs.

And it's easy to keep the separation game going along nicely by blaming our relationship problems on things like a bad upbringing, a dysfunctional family, a non-emotional father, a lack of education, poverty, poor housing, the mother-in-law, bad legal advice, the stock market, losing one's job, bankruptcy, divorce and so on. We all do a great job in this regard. It's just another way to leverage the pain of separation.

Of course, it is possible that romantic love (as Eros) might survive this stage. The same applies to Storge love. It, too, may be strong enough to withstand the strain and keep the family together until that moment you wake up and realize what life is all about. If the love does survive the ordeal, that's fine; but we need to be clear that this was not the goal in the beginning. Relationships are designed by Spirit to be painful and difficult experiences, at least until your soul's need for separation has been satisfied. Only then can Love expand into the fullness of what is possible.

Relationships serve other purposes that are subsidiary to the main two mentioned in the first paragraph of this chapter. The other ways in which relationships serve a purpose are:

1. To Heal Old Wounds
In this chapter, we have already shown how we create separation by using the pain of old wounds to activate core-negative beliefs

and shadow material. But this has a purpose after the awakening as well, in helping you identify and bring to the surface for healing all the old pain, unconscious shadow material and your core negative beliefs. This is dealt with fully later, but suffice it to say here, this would be impossible without having other people to reflect it all back to you. We need relationships.

2. To Be Healing Angels for Each Other

As already mentioned, we need others in our lives to resonate with our own karma and victim consciousness. Only then will we have something to leverage. But in order to feel victimized, we need to attract people into our lives who will do something 'nasty' to us. Then we will have someone to blame and feel resentment towards; and before we know it, we will be in a war with this person or group of people. The relationship so created may be very short-lived, lasting only for a few moments, or it may go on for years, as we have observed in this chapter.

[*To hear me read an article I wrote about how Senator John Edwards might have been a healing angel for his wife Elizabeth by being unfaithful, go to www.ExpandingInLove.com or scan the QR code.*]

Sometimes we play the victim role, while at other times we play the perpetrator role. We have to have both; otherwise, it wouldn't work. On the surface, it will look like we are sworn enemies, and the relationship often gets acted out in this way. It can get very ugly. But the truth is we are soul partners in an enterprise in which the goal, eventually, is for both to awaken and expand into Love. This happens, upon awakening, when we recognize that our enemies are our healing angels, generously providing the means by which to reach that goal.

3. To Fulfill a Soul Agreement

Again, this is dealt with in depth in Chapter 11, so I won't say much about it here except to explain the basic idea. The notion is that we may have made a number of contracts or agreements with certain souls, prior to our incarnation, to do certain things for us or to us at particular times in our life's journey to give us the experiences we want. Obviously, such soul agreements could not be fulfilled without our having the necessary relationship occur in our lifetime.

Once we realize this as a possibility and that we are acting as healing angels for each other by prior agreement, then the purpose for the relationship takes on new meaning. However, this realization only happens after the awakening.

4. To Balance Karmic Energies

Energy of any kind always wants to find its point of equilibrium. It is always seeking balance. This is true of human energy also. We are constantly trying to balance various energies we are holding within us, especially those we create through acting as either victim or perpetrator, whether in this lifetime or another. As we have seen already, during the spiritual amnesia phase when we are concerned with getting karmic units, we will continually find ways to get our energies misaligned and out of balance both within ourselves and with others. In order to leverage that karma, we will attract others into our lives to resonate with those energies and ignite the flames of conflict.

At least it will seem that way. In truth, the Universe is always in perfect balance; and it is through relationship that we offer each other the opportunity to balance out our karmic energies. For example, if we have experienced, either in the current lifetime or a previous one, being the victim of some abuse in order to earn karmic units, we might, in this life, become the abuser for someone else.

That seems a negative formulation, but only if you see it just from the human perspective without any allowance for the spiritual. From the psychological perspective, the person is deeply wounded by the abuse and is acting it out on other 'innocent' people and should first be stopped – and then helped. Of course, that is the truth at the human level. I would do everything I could to stop it, too, because I am human. No one can justify the suffering of others by reference to a spiritual philosophy. To do that is to play God.

But even while we are doing what needs to be done, we can be open to the possibility that there is a spiritual purpose in it somewhere and that some energies are being balanced on both sides. When we are able to see this, it becomes an opportunity to expand into Love because we are seeing it as a call for Love. When we bring Love to the situation, healing happens. No healing occurs when we withhold it, either at the personal level or the collective level. The balancing of energies and the transformation of situations which result from an imbalance can only occur when we are able to experience it fully and then lovingly embrace it as is. Only then will balance be restored.

5. To Help Carry Out Our Mission
It seems to me that life has a purpose to it other than to simply to get a handle on Oneness. I think we agree in advance of our incarnation to do certain things in our life that will give it meaning in real terms and will contribute in some way to the process of 'healing' humanity. More on this topic in Chapter 11. The point here, however, is that it is through relationship that our missions are fulfilled, whatever they are.

[I believe Princess Diana had a mission to open the heart chakra of England and Prince Charles helped her achieve it. To listen to my take on this, go to www.ExpandingInLove.com or scan the QR code.]

3. Relationships Once Awakened

Whereas the purpose of relationships during the amnesia phase is to facilitate the achievement of one's goals for separation and to fulfill our soul agreements, once we have awakened, the purpose of relationships changes dramatically. It now becomes a question of supporting each other in staying awake and expanding into Love.

This is not as easy and straight-forward as it sounds. It is tempting to imagine that once we have begun to remember who we are and to see life through the lens of spiritual perfection, life becomes easy and full of unimaginable joy and our relationships become blissful. While it is true that the potential for perpetual joy and a sense of peacefulness is there, it does not come automatically.

We have to practice it. We have to learn how to accept it and to be in it even when life becomes really challenging. We need tools to help us stay in the vibration we have entered into. We need the help and support of others who are also struggling to stay awake and to be willing to reciprocate when they need support. This is what we mean by the term 'Radical Living.' It's the lifestyle that will support us in this part of our journey.

One of the tasks we need to perform, once we have completed the spiritual amnesia phase and have begun the awakening process, is to go back and clear away all the old energies accumulated during that first phase. This means giving up a lot of stories we have spent years being right about, some of which have been the foundation of our identity. It takes a lot of courage to do this because it raises a very big existential question: "If I am not my story, who am I? How do I define myself if not by my story? If I am not a sexual abuse survivor or an adult child of an alcoholic, or an addict myself, then who am I really?"

For this reason, even though I believe the Alcoholics Anonymous program was divinely inspired and has helped millions of people, I do have a problem with the idea that you come to meetings to declare over and over forever, *"My name is _____, and I am an alcoholic; and I am powerless over my life."* It perpetuates victim consciousness and keeps one addicted to the story. In the days when it was first set up, I'm sure it was appropriate. But if the founders were alive today, given the mass consciousness we have now, they might advocate an approach that doesn't keep people addicted to meetings and being stuck in their story.

In terms of the price we pay for being awakened, we might imagine that in some ways, it was much easier for people who did not awaken until they were on their deathbed. (Until fairly recently, this was the norm for most people. Now people are waking up a lot earlier.)

True, those who did not awaken until the moment of their death may have been living a life of perpetual separation and associated suffering. However, it has to be said that they did not have to face the responsibility for having created all their own dramas and circumstances, like we have to do more or less constantly. They were able to continue their whole life blaming their unhappiness on other people, their upbringing, their parents, their poverty stricken life, the war, their illnesses and so on. We cannot. We have to look ourselves squarely in the face and say we created it all.

44

They did not have to look at their shadow and love those disgusting parts of themselves that they had buried deep down in their unconscious minds. But we do. We have to recognize and come to love those parts of ourselves in order to become authentically whole. We have to accept that when we criticize others, we are seeing ourselves reflected even though it is seldom a pretty sight.

They did not have to examine and undo their negative beliefs, not to mention their prejudices and irrational attitudes; but we are obliged to confront them daily. It takes a lot of humility to do this, and we are not always up to it.

Yes, this is the price we have to pay for being allowed to see the truth. It is not an easy path, and we need a lot of help. Yes, we do have tools which help us stay awake, but we need help from others too. We need relationships that are supportive of our staying awake and remaining in a high vibration even when things get tough. Without those relationships, we may fall back asleep.

Having been in victim consciousness for 15,000 years or so, it is all too easy to fall back into it when life throws something unpleasant in our direction. It is very seductive. And we get plenty of support of the wrong kind from lots of people, the media and, not infrequently, from our family and friends, to go back there.

Bear in mind, too, that our awakening is very tenuous and fragile. We don't, as yet, know the whole truth about spiritual reality. We are convinced that there is one, but because we cannot yet see it or know it fully from direct personal experience, we still have to do what I am doing in this book, which is make up a story about it. These stories form the basis of all religions and spiritual philosophies the world has ever seen.

This is the best we can do at this time, though I do have a feeling that the veil will soon be drawn aside and we will be able to see the spiritual big picture in all its glory. We know our stories are wide of the mark, but insofar as they help us look in the direction of the truth yet to be revealed, they are enough.

But the extent to which we can hold onto our view of how it works will always be challenged by events. For myself, my ability to hold onto the story as I have described it so far in this book, and which forms the basis of the Radical Forgiveness philosophy, is greatly challenged when I see pictures of starving children or hear about the trafficking of women for the sex trade and other terrible stories. When I hear about thousands of people dying in earthquakes or people killing each other in wars over territory and things of this nature, I have to ask myself – how can any of this be perfect in any way at all?

This is when I have to look for help from people who think as I do and who can support me in holding onto the possibility that the hand of God is in there somewhere. Fortunately, I have a wife who can do that for me, and I for her, so we are able to support each other in staying in the Radical Living vibration rather than sinking back into victim consciousness just because we cannot answer that question.

But this raises a very important question for a great many people who have come to this point in their lives. What happens if your partner does not share your world view or is unwilling to grow into a conscious form of loving exchange? The quick answer to the first part of that question is to find friends who do, and spend time with people who are able and willing to give and receive mutual support in staying awake and maintaining a high vibration

[Note: In Appendix # 1 you will find instructions on how to create a Radical Living Support Group that is designed to do just that.]

46

Still there is no doubt that it does make it more of a challenge if your partner does not share your world view, or worse yet, rejects yours out of hand and ridicules you for having it. There is not really a whole lot you can do about it, but you have to resist the temptation to reverse or slow your progress in order to conform to your partner's need to keep you unchanged.

There is no doubt that when you change your vibration and everything that goes along with it, it represents a big challenge to those around you. No one likes you to change because it forces them to consider whether or not they need to change as well. If they are not ready for it, they become agitated. This could apply not just to your partner, but to your children if you have any and other members of your family. Even your workmates might be triggered.

Your only remedy is to do a Radical Forgiveness worksheet, whenever you need to do so, on anyone who is showing hostility, and then love and accept them for being that way. It's the only way to deal with it. And it might just have a positive effect, whereas trying to convince him/her through argument or persuasion will be futile. Surrendering to the situation and then finding your support elsewhere in other types of relationships is the best way to approach this issue.

As far as the second part of the question is concerned, it can be a real challenge if your partner is unwilling to release his/her commitment to the view that one partner needs to dominate the other and then relates to the partner only from this position. Hopefully, your commitment to having a more loving relationship will eventually create some movement from your partner in that direction too. When we reach the point where we are constantly giving out the Love vibration, people around us pick up on it and are attracted to it.

47

On the other hand, if the relationship itself is shaky already and other boundaries are being crossed, in addition to there being little or no sharing of love and/or a profound difference in values, this might give you more reasons to think about renegotiating the relationship in a radical way or ending it. (See Chapter 6.)

If you are not in a relationship at this time and are looking to create a new relationship which is not one-sided, this would be one important requirement to put on your list when you come to do a Radical Manifestation worksheet. (See Chapter 16.)

Love is a Verb
No matter where things stand in your current relationship, or the one that you will create in the future, it is likely that the entire approach to relationship will change once you have awakened. Instead of your relationship being a 'thing' (my relationship), you will begin to see it as a way to relate. In fact, we might say that as you begin relating, the relationship will disappear.

Philosopher and theologian, Martin Buber, (1878 – 1965), talks about an "I-It" relationship where one relates to another as an object, something to be possessed. He contrasts this form of relating to that of "I-Thou." This is radically different from "I-It."

In an "I-Thou" relationship, the "I" does not objectify the other as an "It" but instead becomes aware of having a relationship with the other. To relate to a partner in the way of "I-Thou," is to expand into Love at a very deep level. When and if you simply become Love, the "I' and the "Thou" disappear totally, and you simply love. You are so full of Love that it overflows. You have no choice but to give it. As Karen Taylor Good put it in the title of a song, "Love Is a Verb."

48

[To listen to this song by Karen Taylor-Good, go to www.ExpandingInLove.com, or scan the QR code.]

When we move from love into loving, relating becomes about responding in the moment to the other person's needs and desires while not limiting their freedom to be who they are by demanding they be as negotiated in the kind of relationship 'agreement' we are used to having in a marriage, one that is based on unspoken control and domination. Instead, we consciously decide how we wish to relate to each other, how we can be able to meet our partner's needs and respect his or her boundaries. Out of this arises a deeper level of intimacy, mutual trust and true sharing.

By the way, it is possible that this way of loving can be applied not just to our romantic partners or spouses, but to our children, siblings, parents and other members of our family, friends and neighbors, and even to people we meet only in passing, like the person at the checkout counter in a grocery store, for example.

It has to be said, however, that this does not happen automatically just because you have awakened. In fact, very few people manage to shift from their long established and habitual "I-It" way of relating to an "I-Thou" orientation. It takes effort to break the habit.

Nevertheless, by shifting into this new awareness of who your partner is and by practicing relating to him or her in the way of "I-Thou," it will enable you to expand into a new, more loving relationship, not only with your partner but with yourself, too. You will have infinitely more compassion for yourself and a profound acceptance of who you are, just the way you are.

Again, this is something you have to want and work on creating. It all depends on you, what you want and whether or not you really want to grow. It is your choice, and each moment the choice has to be faced. The tools that will help you expand into Love are provided in this book, so it's not as if you don't have what you need. These tools and processes are tried and tested over many years, and they have been proven to work.

But at least now, the seeds have been planted. The potential is there for the expansion to occur, either with an existing partner – ideally one who is also doing this same work as you – or someone new who wants to relate in this way.

In the following chapters, you will have the opportunity to make an honest assessment of the state of your existing relationship and learn what you can do to expand into the 'I-Thou' way of relating, and how to renegotiate the relationship. If, on the other hand, there seems to be little hope for mutual growth and you are no longer willing to accept a one-sided relationship, then you will find information there which will help you clarify what it is you want that you are not getting now. That way, you will know what to look for in a new relationship should this one come to a timely end.

4. Your Relationship Now

As we noted in the previous chapter, when it comes to relationships, the challenges that arise after we have awakened are not much different to how they were before. However, instead of using them to create separation as we did then, we now use the relationship to grow and expand in Love.

By the way, just in case you are wondering, expanding in Love does not necessarily require romantic love (Eros) to be present. The same applies to Storge love, the kind that is founded on familiarity and the enjoyment of each other's company. Though it's nice if one or both are present, neither one is a prerequisite. That's because expanding in Love is all about the expansion of your own capacity to see the perfection in God's creation just the way it is, even if you don't like it. That's what Love is, and that's what we need to do to expand into it.

It is even possible for two people who thoroughly dislike each other to expand in Love through their mutual interactions. So long as they actively relate one to another with honesty, integrity, generosity, caring and mutual respect, they will expand their capacity to love. If they are able to relate without projecting, making demands, holding expectations or making unfair judgments, their manner of relating will be one of I-Thou, which, as Martin

Buber pointed out, is a much higher level of relating than I-It, that being the kind of relationship most people create.

I would suggest that the two people disliking each other but relating in an I-Thou way have much more authentic Love in that relationship than most people. It will probably be rather dull, but since neither one controls the other, they each can find excitement outside of their relationship. On the other hand, I can imagine this kind of relationship existing between two soldiers having to fight side by side in battle and not liking each other, yet bonding in a way that is deep and meaningful. Such a relationship is unlikely to be boring.

I make this point now because I know that many people are reading this book because they have a relationship that is not going super well; and while they would like to get some tips on how to make it work better, they worry that the Love is not really there. "How can I expand in Love if there's none there to start with?" they might ask.

Again, this misses the point. Expanding in Love is about increasing your *capacity* to love, and that means being able to accept people just the way they are. It just so happens that relationships offer the opportunity to learn how to achieve this, no matter how good or bad the relationships seem to be.

Assessing Your Relationship
On the website for members of The Radical Living Online Community is an online worksheet that is extremely helpful in making an analysis of your current relationship (or a previous one if you are not currently in one), in order to see how it can help you expand into Love. You would need to join the Association to have access to it (as well as many other online tools); but as an awakened person trying to master the Radical Living lifestyle, I cannot

imagine why you would not. The cost is minimal, and the tools are extremely valuable.

*[For details and to become a member of the **Radical Living Online Community**, scan the QR code or go to www.colintipping.com/membership.]*

The reason I have put this instrument of inquiry there rather than in the pages of this book with a lot of places provided where you would fill in details of your relationship, is that I realized it would be risky for you to write such intimate and private information in a book that others might easily pick up and read. Much better that it be online so you will have it properly protected by passwords, etc. The online worksheet is more interactive and more user friendly that can be provided in a book, so it is better all around to do it this way.

When you login to the worksheet, it will ask you to examine how you feel about your relationship now compared to how you felt at the beginning and to make an assessment of how your partner would answer the same question. It will ask you to assess the strength and quality of your love now, as in eros, philia and storge, compared to when you first fell in love, and to assess how your partner might answer that one too. Based on that information, it will suggest you write a short description of your relationship as it exists at this time. You will then be invited to assess your relative satisfaction/dissatisfaction levels and to gauge your partner's. What your thoughts were about him/her at the time of your coming together in a committed relationship and what your thoughts are now are other areas of inquiry that you will find interesting and revealing. Recalling what expectations, judgments, assumptions, demands and values you both brought to the relationship will also be enlightening.

The worksheet gives you a lot of help answering such questions. In many cases, it gives you multiple choices and examples for you to examine and put a check mark by; so it makes it easy and even, to some degree, fun. It need not take very long to actually do it, but it will give you a lot of food for thought. Remember, the objective is to use the information in a way that will help you expand in Love. It is not about blaming anyone or making anyone wrong. That's the old paradigm. Remember there are no mistakes.

It would be ideal if your partner were willing to participate with you in this inquiry and be open to giving his or her own answers to the questions on the worksheet. If not, then you will need to make your own private assessment of how you think your partner might answer them.

If you plan to do this inquiry together, you will need to set up a way of doing it that suits you both. For example, decide whether you will do it together at the same time or whether each of you will do it separately. You would also need to decide when to get back together to share the responses and then make an agreement about how that discussion would need to proceed.

If you are already a member of the Radical Living Online Community, login now and take the time to go through this process of assessing your relationship. I think you will find it an enlightening experience.

[To log in, scan the QR code to go to the Login Page or go to www.radicalforgiveness. member.]

Prenuptial Agreements

We usually associate prenuptials with rich people needing to make some agreement over how their wealth would be split up in the event of divorce. Though I do think people ought to be very open with each other going into a relationship regarding money, and should discuss in detail how it will be shared and managed etc., that's not the kind of prenuptial agreement I am talking about here.

When my wife, JoAnn, and I decided to get married, we had a friend who came round to our house, sat us down and went through a list of questions that were designed to uncover all our unspoken assumptions and expectations, as well as things we had never thought about or had even asked ourselves before. Bringing all that up to the surface for discussion was the most useful thing we did for our future together. It gave us a lot of clarity about how we each envisioned the relationship. Where there was some divergence of priority or disagreement over something, we had to hammer it out. This has been the foundation for our relationship for the last 22 years.

However, looking back now, it seems clear to me that we both entered that relationship having done enough work on ourselves to think that we were in the awakened phase and that we did this as a way to avoid using this relationship as a way to create separation. Both of us had done that before in previous marriages.

What you hopefully have had the opportunity to do with the online worksheet is to do the same inquiry from the perspective of an awakened person. Assuming that, from now on, you have an interest in expanding your capacity to love using the relationship as the vehicle, going over all those questions with your partner and using them to initiate a conversation will prove to be very beneficial.

But again let me remind you that, should it be the case that you have fallen out of love, the goal is not necessarily that you fall back in love with each other. Nor is it about getting agreements from your partner, at least not at this stage. It is not even about whether you stay together or not. The extent to which you expand in Love will be the degree to which you enter the process in a state of trust and willingness to accept and surrender to whatever outcome emerges out of the process knowing that, without a doubt, that's how it should be. I'm not saying this is easy to achieve, but it's your best chance of finding peace and moving forward into an expanded Love.

It's also your best chance of saving the relationship if you so desire and perhaps finding a deeper Love for each other than has ever been possible before. Even if you are in the process of separating and have no interest in saving the relationship, both of you will benefit by doing this inquiry, in that this self knowledge will help you in creating your next relationship. Knowledge is power, but self-knowledge is wisdom.

Did You Settle?
This is another interesting question to ask yourself. It is not unusual for people to go into a relationship that looks perfect in the beginning while both parties are on their best behavior and are wearing masks, and then come to find after about 6 months that their prospective partner has some serious problems. This is how long it takes for these problems to show up because real intimacy (INTO-ME-SEE) takes that amount of time to develop. All of a sudden, the union begins to look like an impending disaster.

However, instead of pulling out and avoiding that trap, they go ahead with it, for a number of reasons, just hoping it will be OK. Among the many reasons they do this, one is to avoid disappointing that partner and/or his or her family (co-dependence) by backing out, not wanting to say "NO," feeling stupid for having made a big thing about this person being their soul mate, etc.

However, the primary reason they hang in there is because their need for a relationship is stronger than their misgivings about the relationship. In other words, they sell themselves out just so they can have a relationship, no matter how bad it might be. They go into denial, pretend not to notice the problems in the relationship and make believe it is OK. Women especially indulge in an even worse kind of denial by telling themselves, "If I love him enough, he will change." I hear that one all the time.

[To watch a video of me explaining this using a flip chart, go to www.expandinginlove.com, or scan the QR code.]

Did You Marry Your Parent of the Opposite Sex?

If you had issues with the parent of the opposite sex it is highly likely that you will have attracted someone much like your mother or father to be in relationship with. It's that leverage dynamic again.

If it is the case that you have unresolved childhood wounds and/or forgiveness issues with that parent, someone who is just like him or her will be attracted to you and will resonate with the energy of that wound. You will then play out the wound with your partner as if he or she were that parent. It is virtually a given, for example, that a girl who grew up with a Dad who was alcoholic will find a partner with that addiction. The solution is to forgive your Dad.

[If this applies, check out the online program, "Breaking Free," a 21-Day Program for Forgiving Your Parents. Scan here to learn more or go to www.colintipping.com/online-programs.]

Who Controls the Relationship?

In every relationship, especially during the period when creating separation is the main purpose of getting together, one partner predominantly controls the relationship. There may be some areas and roles in which the controller has voluntarily ceded control to the other, but mostly it holds true that one partner will dominate.

In our society, it is still predominantly the male partner who dominates since that is the nature of masculine energy. Female energy is more receptive, open and responsive. Where a woman does tend to dominate she will likely possess a fair amount of masculine energy about her and will, if the relationship is to work reasonably well, attract a male partner who has feminine energy in roughly the same proportion. "She's the one who wears the trousers," is a way of expressing this power arrangement.

We could also say that the partner who has the least sex drive controls the relationship. The one with the highest need for sex must continue to court the other partner in the hope that the favor may be granted, if not now, then at some time in the future. Even if they act powerfully in other ways in the relationship, if sex is important to them, their having to plead for sex, or at worst demand sex whether the other wants it or not, automatically puts them in a subservient position. For some, it can be extremely demeaning.

Another way that one partner can control the other is through money. There are still some men who will never tell their wives how much they earn or how much they have in the bank. Either partner can also make it so the other is dependent on them financially in a number of ways, making the other feel they don't have the freedom to spend money in the way they want to without asking permission, or that they would not be able to leave the relationship because they would be severely disadvantaged if they were to do so.

It is interesting that the two main causes of relationship breakdown are issues around money and sex. In her book, *The Anatomy of Spirit*, Caroline Myss proposes that the energies associated with both money and sex tend to settle in the Sacral Chakra.

Chakras are energy centers within the etheric body. The etheric body is the energy body that exists one octave higher in vibration than the physical body (which is also an energy body, but which vibrates at a sufficiently low frequency that it manifests as physical form).

Fig. 2: The Chakra System

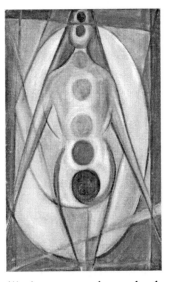

There are seven chakras in the Etheric Body, and each one is energetically connected to specific glands and organs in the physical body; so even though the chakras are energetic in nature, they do have an effect on the physical body.

According to Caroline Myss, since the issues we have around sex or money tend to settle in the second chakra, the Sacral Chakra, these energies are likely to create specific physical symptoms.

Money issues, for example, often will show up as lower back problems. Sexual issues will manifest not only as pain in the lumbar region but as problems with the entire reproductive system. Women are affected most, obviously, but men, too, will find themselves 'aborting' ideas and creating blocks to their creative energies.

From an emotional standpoint, guilt, especially guilt around sex, is located in this sacral chakra. Failure to process this emotion often shows up as excess weight around the hips and lower abdomen. Ethical issues, especially as they relate to relationships are implicated in this chakra. Fidelity would fall into that category.

The point here is that your body is a good indicator of what is, or has been, going on with you emotionally. It also will tell you who you need to forgive now that you have awakened to the truth and have begun the process of clearing the energies back along the timeline. If you are having lower back problems, you would need to look at your money issues first and then your sex life. It also might mean that your creativity is being blocked in some way, either within the relationship or at work perhaps.

Sacral Chakra issues are showing up in my relationship in the following way: _____

_____

_____

Looking now at Chakra #1, **the Root Chakra,** if you have problems in your body from the hip area down to the feet, including lower colon, prostate, genitals and bladder, ask yourself how you are being made to feel unsafe or insecure. Who is, or has been, responsible for making you feel this way and undermining your very foundation? Problems with legs and feet may indicate a desire to run or a feeling of not being able to move forward in your life. Another issue revealed in this first chakra is the tendency not to stand up for yourself when attacked, especially by a father figure or someone who assumes authority over you.

Root Chakra issues are showing up in my relationship in the following way: _____

_____

_____

Problems in the area of Chakra #3, the **Solar Plexus Chakra,** will manifest as stomach problems, adrenals, liver and digestive issues, and mid-back pain. If you have any of these bodily symptoms, these may well be indicating that you are dealing with issues of personal power, control and self-esteem. So, look to see if power

60

struggles or control issues have figured in your relationships, not only with your partner but with other people as well, especially your mother. My experience is that mothers often tend to exert control energetically through this chakra. Look also to see whether your partner has treated you in a way that has kept your self-esteem fairly low. Co-dependence is also located in this chakra.

Solar Plexus Chakra issues are showing up in my relationship in the following way: _____

_____

_____

Energies that settle in the **Heart Chakra** (#4) will represent issues around love, hate, jealousy, resentment, forgiveness (or lack thereof), and associated pain arising from a 'broken heart.' Mid to upper-back problems, heart problems, pulmonary issues and problems in the breast and chest area will arise if there is energy stuck in this chakra. Whenever I meet someone with breast cancer, I always ask, *"Who broke your heart between 5 to 7 years before the onset of the cancer?"* They can come up with a name almost without thinking, and a light bulb usually goes on immediately.

Heart Chakra issues are showing up in my relationship in the following way: _____

_____

_____

Chakra #5 is the **Throat Chakra.** This covers the shoulders, the thyroid, neck, mouth, teeth and throat. Problems connected to difficulties with communication and personal expression will show up here. Not being able to speak your truth will produce symptoms in this area, especially sore throats and thyroid problems. Secrets

61

are also highly toxic too and will produce physical symptoms. This is also the chakra which holds the energy of will and the ability to make things happen through the power of the word. Stiff or aching shoulders can be associated with having to 'shoulder' too much responsibility. Power and control are easily achieved over one's partner by what one says, or what one does not say, so this chakra is very important. Silence is a powerful weapon.

Throat Chakra issues are showing up in my relationship in the following way: _____

_____

Chakra #6, **the Third Eye** is about your own self-awareness, your intuition and your connection to truth. The energy of this chakra affects the eyes and ears, your nervous system, the brain and the pineal gland. If your partner is inclined to ridicule your intuitive abilities and your spiritual connection, this could be a problem.

Third Eye Chakra issues are showing up in my relationship in the following way: _____

_____

The Crown Chakra (#7) is located at the top of the head and is all about your life values, your faith, your trust in life, your connection to God and being able to see the big picture. Any energetic block in this chakra shows up in the skin and muscles.

Crown Chakra issues are showing up in my relationship in the following way: _____

It is also interesting to note how Myss links the chakras to the way we have been evolving spiritually over the centuries. Up until quite recently, we all tended to live in our lower three chakras since these three are all to do with family and tribe. The principal value is loyalty to the group and obedience to the social order as prescribed by the tribe. Individual wants and needs are subservient to the needs of the group.

As we have evolved socially and spiritually, we have tried moving into the heart chakra and living from that space of *"What about me?"* It is a risky space, and we get heavily criticized and even punished by the group for putting ourselves above the needs of the group. Then, as we move into the throat chakra, we begin to speak our own personal truth and begin acting out of our own will rather than the group will. We become empowered to make our own decisions and to live our own dreams. As we move into the 6th chakra, we find our own ability to connect to our own Spiritual Intelligence and then, through the crown chakra, to make a personal connection with the God of our own understanding rather than the one given by the tribe.

This shift from tribal loyalty to individual power, is somewhat analogous to the shift we have already talked about from the old paradigm to the new one. Paradigm #1 has a commitment to the mass mindset of a tribal-reinforced victim consciousness while Paradigm #2 is about being awake and self-aware. This is especially true when we move into the 6th and 7th chakra. This is where we begin to operate not just from our mental and emotional intelligence (as from our heart chakra) but from our Spiritual Intelligence as well. When we are operating from the Crown Chakra, we really begin to see the big picture and become fully awake.

5. Practical Considerations

Having done all this analysis, the question then becomes, what do you do with all this information? The answer is nothing – at least not yet. Under normal circumstances, you would use the information to re-negotiate the terms of the relationship and to fix the problems as you saw them. You might even hire yourself a therapist to help you do this.

But as we suggested in Chapter 2, a relationship based on bargaining and a 'negotiated' love would only result in returning to the I-It way of relating. This is where each person in the relationship objectifies the other and ends up dominating or being dominated. This was perfect for when the goal was to create experiences of separation, but it is not the way to grow a relationship once we have awakened. The objective is to take it to the I-Thou level that Martin Buber talks about. So how do we do that?

The first thing is to remember that you created this relationship for a reason. As a soul-to-soul arrangement, either as a pre-incarnation agreement or one that came about during this lifetime through the law of resonance, it was what you wanted. You and your partner are literally soul mates.

Note: I do not use the term 'soul mates' in the way that most people use it as a way to describe an especially romantic relationship with a divine connection. We are ALL soul mates for each other as soon as we come into relationship, no matter whether the relationship lasts a couple of minutes or 20 years. Every relationship, no matter how good or bad it seems, is a soul-to-soul transaction.

So this is the point from which we must proceed if we are to take our ability to love to the next level. We need to see that the relationship was, from the beginning and right up to this point (assuming you are still in it), perfect in every way. I know it might not look like it at the moment, and perhaps from a human perspective, it is not; but that is old paradigm thinking.

When I said that you should do nothing with all this information, I did not mean you should not take action. I just meant for you to avoid doing what most people do, and what most therapists would have you do (unless, of course, they were Radical Forgiveness practitioners or coaches), which is to try to fix the relationship.

Neither would I want you to make any decisions about whether to stay or leave the relationship (assuming that was on your mind). Better that you wait until you have done some expanding in Love exercises first before you make this decision, assuming the option still remains.

The ONLY action I would ask you to take right now is to do one or more Radical Acceptance Worksheets. (See page 72) This is similar to a Radical Forgiveness Worksheet, but it focuses not on what your partner may have done to upset you but on seeing him/her as he/she really is. The worksheet is designed to help you come to a place of acceptance of him/her as a divine being whose perfection, for you, lies in his/her imperfection.

If there is some forgiveness called for over something specific he/ she has done, you should do as many Radical Forgiveness worksheets as necessary to dissolve the energy around each hurtful act. I would recommend the Online Radical Forgiveness Worksheet on the Radical Living Online Community membership site for this, though free worksheets are also available.

[Scan here to go to www.colintipping.com/ membership to find the online worksheets for members as well as the free worksheets for anyone.]

Just doing the worksheets might change everything without you doing anything else. That's why I said you should not do any re-negotiation of the relationship until you have done the worksheets and allowed time for its effect to settle into your and your partner's consciousness. It is, after all, a principle that whatever is occurring 'out there' is a reflection of what's 'in here.' In other words, however your relationship looks is an outplaying of your own consciousness. Once you change your consciousness, the situation 'out-there' is bound to change.

As you do the worksheets, you will be asking your Spiritual Intelligence to help you release all the old habits of the old paradigm and begin relating with your partner from the new paradigm. That will be all that is necessary. If you get busy trying to negotiate and redefine the relationship, you would just get in the way. You would be going back to the old paradigm way of relating.

Doing this worksheet will shift the energy in you quite quickly, but it may take some time before you and your partner begin relating differently; so you will have to be patient. It might take a while to go from a lifetime habit of relating to each other in the I-It mode to the I-Thou mode. Just be observant and notice the changes that do occur over time.

Obviously, it will happen more quickly and more profoundly if both of you are doing this work together; but if your partner is totally resistant to changing, then the relationship itself comes into question and you may have a decision to make. Nevertheless, the work you will have done in coming to accept him/her will make this decision so much easier; and if you do have to separate, you will be able to use even that experience to expand in Love. Isn't that a novel idea!

This brings me to the trickiest question of all. How do we gauge whether to leave or stay in the relationship? The debate comes down to whether it may have achieved its original purpose and run its course or whether there might still be more good growth opportunities to be had from staying with it?

The fact is that it is often the breakdown of a marriage or significant relationship which brings us to that point of awakening, so it may be too late anyway. It may already be over for you. But since this chapter is still about assessing an existing relationship, let's assume you are still in the relationship even though it does not seem great and you are being challenged with that question - to leave or not to leave.

In the 60's when divorce started to become more acceptable, Susan Gettleman and Janet Markowitz wrote a book called, *The Courage to Divorce*. It gave people 'permission' to make that choice if that's what they wanted. The effect of this relaxing of the rules of engagement, so to speak, has been that people tend now to jump out of a marriage very quickly when things get a little difficult and, consequently, miss the opportunity to grow through the pain. Instead of using the relationship to get their karmic units, and eventually awaken as a result of it, they avoid the pain and then have to find someone else with whom to finish off the process. That's not to say this is wrong (there are no accidents or mistakes), but it does seem to cry out for another book entitled, "The Courage

NOT to Divorce." Such a book would speak to the above dilemma and would at least suggest that people should ask themselves that question.

But to be honest, in the way that it is framed, it is really an unanswerable question. How could we know what Spirit has in store for us in this relationship in the future? And how would we know what would follow if we left? We just don't know. However, as we have indicated, one of the advantages of being awake and being in alignment with the new paradigm is that we don't have to know these things. Trying to figure it out is a waste of time. If we trust and surrender to the process and stay alive to guidance from our Spiritual Intelligence, we will be shown what to do. And if we seem to make a mistake, that will be perfect too.

Had we still been in the spiritual amnesia phase, we would simply use the divorce, if it were to occur, as just another way to feel more separation. That would be perfect, especially if it precipitated the awakening as I have already pointed out. But now that we have the spiritual awareness of how our current relationship might give us the opportunity to expand in Love in a way that would raise our consciousness, we might think twice before we abandon it. If we left and had to start all over again, it could take a lot longer. After all, it is very unwise to begin a new relationship within a year or two of leaving the last one since you are likely to take a lot of the old energy of the last one into the new one. And that would add a lot of confusion.

The real answer to this dilemma is simple. Stop trying to figure it out. Exercise trust and surrender by doing the Radical Acceptance, Radical Forgiveness and Radical Self-Acceptance Worksheets. Your Spiritual Intelligence will take care of the details. The worksheets and other downloadable audio versions of them along with online programs are listed in Appendix I in the back of this book. You have plenty of resources to employ that will bring you to a place of peace. When you find that kind of calm space, I can assure you, clarity about what to do next will come to you.

Using a therapist can help, but please avoid any that are still using the medical model embedded in the old paradigm. Use a practitioner who is trained in Radical Forgiveness Therapy.

[Information about how to find one can be found at www.colintipping.com/coaching. Scan this QR Code to go directly to the list of coaches.]

When you have reached a place of peace through doing this process and have decided that you wish to continue with the relationship and have the intention to use it as a way to expand in Love, you can begin to converse with your partner about how this can be achieved.

If your partner has been doing the work as well as you, either separately or together, and is ready to go to the next step of using the relationship to expand in Love, that will be an advantage. If you have been doing this process on your own and your partner is still committed to the old paradigm, then it will be more difficult. Here you can make an assessment of the situation:

☐ My partner has more or less the same consciousness as me.

☐ My partner is open to my way of thinking but remains skeptical for himself/herself.

☐ My partner tolerates my way of thinking but is not open to it for himself/herself.

☐ My partner is critical and judgmental of my way of thinking and completely rejects it.

☐ My partner is scornful of my thinking and becomes very angry about it.

You might be tempted to think that the more your partner is resistant to your way of thinking, the more obvious it becomes that moving on and finding someone else who is more in alignment with your consciousness would be the best solution. Maybe, or maybe not.

Of course, it would be nice to have someone as a partner who is of the same mind as you, but it would not necessarily cause you to expand in Love. Someone who ridicules your way of thinking or attacks your beliefs offers a much more challenging proposition than someone who agrees with you. It would force you to expand in Love in order to come to a place of unconditional acceptance of him or her, no matter how strong the attack and irrespective of his/

Fig. 3: The Radical Acceptance Worksheet
This worksheet is most helpful when you find a person very diffi-cult to accept as he or she is. Projection may well be involved as well, of course. If so, you should recognize the opportunity to take it back and be thankful for the mirroring. However, Radical Acceptance goes beyond having a judgment about someone. You will feel it as wanting the person be different.

As you go through the worksheet you will be reminded that ev-eryone is as God has made them and that they being the way they are because that is who they are. However, accepting some-one is not the same as liking them. Liking is not a requirement; only that you find it possible to see the Christ in them, knowing that we are all One.

A mock Radical Acceptance Worksheet is shown on the next page but it is also offered on the Radi-cal Living Online Community website as an online interactive worksheet. Scan the QR code or go to *www.radicalforgiveness.com/member* for it.

Radical Acceptance

A *Tipping Method* Worksheet for Seeing the Divinity in Any Human Being

1. I recognize that I am finding it difficult to accept _____ as he/she is. The problem I have with him/her is:

2. The main feelings I am experiencing within myself right now as I bring this person to mind are: *(be totally honest and use feeling words.)*

3. I honor my feelings and claim my right, as an awakened human being, to experience emotions and to be responsive to them. I value them because they give me good feedback about how I am seeing this person. ☐ **AGREE** ☐ **DISAGREE**

4. Even though I am not aware of what it might be, I am open to the possibility that this person is in my life for a reason and possibly is here to provide me a lesson or healing opportunity. ☐ **AGREE** ☐ **DISAGREE**

5. I recognize that I may be using this person to not only create some fresh pain of separation within myself, but also to leverage one or more similar instances of separation between myself and other important people in my life. For example:

I am therefore recognizing in this person, from whom I have withheld love and have judged, a soul-mate on a mission to awaken me to the truth of who I truly am, who he/she is, and who those are from whom I have withheld love previously. We are all part of the one Divine Essence. ☐ **AGREE** ☐ **DISAGREE**

6. Even though I know there is no requirement that I like this individual as a human being, nor approve his/her behavior in human terms, I am now willing to see the light in him/her and to know that the person's soul is Love, pure and simple and he/she is, therefore, perfect in every way. ☐ **AGREE** ☐ **DISAGREE**

7. I am feeling a sense of Oneness with this person now and feel gratitude for this person being in my life. ☐ **AGREE** ☐ **DISAGREE**

Signed: _____ Date: _____

her own belief system. The way to cope with this scenario and get the best out of it is to do a Radical Acceptance Worksheet and then continue working on you.

In the old paradigm, victim consciousness was sustained by many structures and ways of interacting with each other. One of them was the 'attack and defense cycle.' Whenever we felt we were being attacked, we naturally felt the need to defend ourselves by attacking in return. The attack and defense cycle is formalized and enshrined in the activity of war. The challenge for us in the new paradigm is to break that cycle by responding to an attack, not with aggression and revenge but with Love. If we meet aggression with Love, the energy behind the attacker collapses. Love is the only real defense.

As it says in *A Course in Miracles*, "My strength and power lies in my vulnerability." This is totally contrary to how we normally think, but it is based on the example lived by Jesus. Jesus was Love. Love is how Gandhi came to defeat the might of the great British Empire machine and brought it to its knees. Martin Luther King met terrible violence with non-violence and established civil rights for blacks in America. Mother Teresa could stop the war in Lebanon for a day with her Love. These were the real spiritual giants of history, not the political leaders who wanted war for their own glory.

There is a tendency for people who have reached the point of having an awakened awareness, to imagine that they are more 'evolved' than those who have not. I hear a lot of spiritual people lament the fact that their partner is "not yet on his/her spiritual path," and that this has become a real problem for them. I'm afraid I get a little upset with them about this.

The fact is, of course, that everyone is on their spiritual path. There isn't anyone who is not. Everyone is where they are supposed to be. Maybe they chose to shoot for more karmic units than the other person did and still have more to go yet before awakening. Who knows what the truth is, but it is not for us to make judgments about where we think they are along the path.

Your first step in expanding in Love, therefore, is in recognizing that no matter where your partner is in terms of consciousness, he/she is exactly where he/she is meant to be. And so are you.

We also need to consider the possibility that your partner's resistance is mirroring your own inability to live the new paradigm as authentically as you might wish to. Your own doubts might be being reflected back to you, in which case his or her behavior is his/her gift to you. If that is so, the moment you allow that in as a possibility and you begin to feel a sense of loving gratitude for him/her bringing that to your awareness, the attacks will very likely stop. The purpose for them will have been served. As you recognize your partner as your 'healing angel,' you not only forgive him/her, but you automatically forgive yourself. That's how it works.

It's an energy thing. The biologist, Rupert Sheldrake, has demonstrated how people are connected energetically within what he called morphogenetic fields. If one person within the field changes his/her vibratory rate, this has an effect throughout the whole field.

[To watch a video that explains this dynamic, go to www.expandinginlove.com, or scan the QR code.]

The stronger the link between individual members within that field, the more potent this effect becomes. No matter what the state of your relationship might be at this moment, the energetic link between you and your partner must still be very strong.

If you respond to your partner's attack, not by counter-attacking but by sending only Love, your partner cannot help but be affected. You will also have raised your vibration by doing so. Beforehand, there would have been a sort of energetic equilibrium, even if the energy was blocked.

As soon as you raise your vibration and expand in Love, he/she must respond in order to restore the energetic balance. More often than not, the person responds by automatically raising his/her vibration and expanding in Love themselves. At that point, it is possible that the block dissolves and the energy of acceptance (Love) begins to flow again.

> *[You will find this much easier to grasp seeing it explained on video, so scan the QR code or go to www.ExpandingInLove.com to see me give the presentation.]*

All this happens way below the level of consciousness, of course, but the effects can be dramatic, observable and immediate. On the other hand, they can also be subtle and take some time to become evident.

The important thing here, though, is that you don't fall into the trap of doing the work of expanding in Love simply in order to get such results. That would be just another form of manipulation and exploitation, and it would not work. You should have no expectation in this regard. Just continue expanding your capacity to love what is, as is, in order to find peace within yourself.

None of what we have said up to now precludes your leaving the relationship if that would seem the sensible thing to do. No one is suggesting you stay in the relationship if it is abusive, toxic or in any other way intolerable. Since this work is all about energy, which is not subject to the limitations of time and space, there is nothing of this work that can't be done while at a distance.

So, if the conditions are such that to maintain your physical presence in the relationship is simply too much to bear and you feel you need to separate from your partner, be assured that the power of doing the work is not in any way diminished. Your job is still to come to a place where you can accept your partner just the way he/she is and see him/her as a soul who has come into your life for a reason and who loves you unconditionally.

But again, this does not mean you have to put up with unacceptable behavior. Nor does it preclude your having boundaries of your own or wanting to have a workable set of agreements. You don't even have to like someone for this to work. It is a matter of you being able to see beyond the personality and recognize the divinity in the person. That will stop you going into the attack/defense cycle, and enable you to go to the Love vibration instead. However, you definitely need the tools to help you do that. The Radical Acceptance Worksheet will take you to that place, but here's a version of the Emerge-n-See, 4-Step Process that will also come in handy in the moment. (More on this in Chapter 11.)

1. Look What a Relationship I've Co-created with this Person.

2. I Notice My Judgments and Feelings but Love Myself Anyway.

3. I am willing to Expand My Love by Accepting Him/Her Just the Way He/She Is.

4. I Choose Peace and Love.

You may have to say this to yourself a few times to get to a place where you can feel the peace and, perhaps, even come to glimpse a bit of the divinity in the other person. I would certainly suggest you commit this 4-step process to memory so it comes immediately to mind as soon as you find yourself being overly defensive.

You cannot expand in Love if you are holding onto to any unhealed grievances that were rooted in the relationship. Neither can you engage in any renegotiation of the relationship, nor even create a good ending of the relationship, should that be in the cards, until that energy is dispersed. I urge you, therefore, as part of your work in expanding in Love to do as many Radical Forgiveness worksheets as necessary in order to clear that energy out before attempting to do either.

Exercise:
a) Committing to Radical Forgiveness:
I recognize that I am holding onto some residual anger resentment and sadness towards my partner which is tied to some things that happened while we were in the spiritual amnesia phase of our relationship that made me feel victimized. Since I wish to expand in Love, I, therefore, resolve to do a Radical Forgiveness Worksheet on each of the following grievances, in order to clear my energy field before I begin to re-negotiate my relationship.

1. _____

2. _____

3. _____

4. _____

b) Committing to Radical Self-Forgiveness
I recognize that I am holding onto some residual guilt and shame about myself; and that even though what happened to make me feel this way occurred during the spiritual amnesia phase, I still harbor the guilt and shame around it.

[You may wish to watch a video that makes clear the distinction clear guilt and shame and how they relate to each other. Scan the QR code. or go to www.ExpandingInLove.com.]

Since I wish to expand in Love, I, therefore, resolve to do a Radical Self-Forgiveness Worksheet on each of the following situations, in order to clear my energy field before I begin to renegotiate my relationship.

1. _____

2. _____

3. _____

4. _____

In the two chapters that follow, we will look first at how we can renegotiate the relationship, having first done the energy work, and second, how we can expand in Love even if the relationship is coming to an end and you are likely to be separating.

6. Renegotiating the Relationship

I said earlier that trying to renegotiate the relationship without first doing the energy work on the relationship was rather futile and a waste of energy. It would most likely lead you both straight back into the attack and defense cycle as your strategy for dealing with conflict, which wouldn't be good. It would also reinforce the old habits of holding expectations, making demands, wanting control and being co-dependent. That, of course, would put you back in the old paradigm and the 'I-It' form of relating.

But more than that, it would be silly because doing the energy work first would, more than likely, dissolve most of the problems that existed before anyway. Once we realize that the problems of the past were there in order to help each other feel separate, then we will see them for what they were and have no reason to even discuss them anymore, let alone see them as problems. Therefore, from this point on, the renegotiation needs to be almost exclusively about the future, not the past.

Reciprocity
Up to this point, the discussion has been exclusively about you doing the work of expanding into Love. There has been no requirement that your partner do any of this work for himself or

herself. However, when it comes to renegotiating the relationship, then clearly some reciprocity is required. At the very least, your partner needs to be engaged and committed to working on the relationship with you. Whereas forgiveness is done by the forgiver alone and requires no reciprocity, the process of renegotiation or reconciliation cannot work without it.

Hopefully, as a result of all that you have done to expand in Love and how it has affected him/her, your partner's energy might be much more open than it would have been had you not used the tools and done the work. Nevertheless, if that is not the case and he/she is not really in alignment with you spiritually and is still coming from the old paradigm, don't worry. He/she may well still want to play according to the rules of the old paradigm, at least for a while, because that is all he/she knows.

The difference is that you will play along ONLY to the extent that it supports him/her, but at the same time, you will quietly refuse to be drawn back into the old energy. In other words, you won't get tricked into going into the 'attack and defense' cycle but will send back only Love when you see an attack coming.

When you see him/her projecting onto you, you won't take it personally and you won't react—except with Love. In this way, you will get to practice expanding in Love and feeling radical acceptance of him/her. If you do this, he/she will quite likely come around to your way of thinking even if it is unconscious. Having said that, though, it will still be necessary for you to establish rules for the relationship and set boundaries for yourself.

Even if you both have come to a place of being totally accepting and having no expectations or demands of each other, you will still need to have an understanding of how the relationship needs to work. That level of understanding would not come from a need to dominate and control, however. Rather it would arise naturally out of that 'I-Thou' form of loving which only asks for respect and caring from the other. That's how you need to approach the negotiation process going forward.

Playing By the Rules

One very useful way to have a discussion without it degenerating into an argument or creating an attack-defense cycle, developed by Harville Hendrix, author of *Getting the Love You Want,* is where you each agree to follow a specific set of rules. These are:

You set aside an appropriate amount of time and sit opposite each other so that eye contact is possible. Partner A goes first, saying what is true for him/her, while Partner B simply listens and does not speak. After a while, say after about 5 minutes, Partner A pauses and asks Partner B to reflect back what he/she just said.

Partner B begins by saying, "What I think I heard you say was . . ." and proceeds to reflect back as accurately as possible what he/she thinks was said. He or she must not respond to what is said or say anything other than what he/she heard.

If Partner B was not accurate in his/her reflection, Partner A will say, "No, that's not quite what I said. What I said was . . ." Partner B reflects it again until Partner A is satisfied that he/she has been heard and acknowledged.

He or she will then continue in this way for as long as it takes to finish what he/she needs to say at that point. Partner B asks, "Are you complete?" Partner A says, "Yes."

Now it's Partner B's turn to speak while Partner A listens and reflects back. This back and forth way of communicating goes on until the conversation is complete, with each partner taking care always to retain ownership of how they are seeing the situation or feeling about it. This is achieved by always beginning with an "I" statement. "I am feeling . . ." or "The way I see it is . . ."

Never begin with a "you" statement, such as "You told me . . ." Rather we would say, "My recollection of the conversation was . . ."

This approach will help you stay out of the attack/defense cycle, but both partners must stick to the rules if it is to work. Once the back and forth sharing has come to an end, it is best to simply say "thank you," and leave it at that for a moment or two before broadening it out as a discussion of what was shared. Do your best not to let it become an argument by sticking to the method of each one listening and reflecting back.

[To see this couples communication system being demonstrated live on video, scan the QR code or go to www.ExpandingInLove.com.]

Boundaries

It is a measure of your respect for both your partner and yourself that, during your discussions, you let your partner know where your limits are in terms of what you will accept and what you won't. These often rise to the level of principle and are reflective of your own sense of self as an individual and how you wish to be treated in the relationship. Some of them may even rise to the level of 'deal killers' in the sense that the relationship would not survive if they were dishonored or crossed.

However, it is incumbent upon you to really give deep consideration to what your boundaries and limits might be at this time. [See below for some discussion points relating to boundaries.] They may be quite different to how they were before you shifted to the new paradigm. At that time, you might have wanted to be treated in disrespectful ways, or even abusive ways, in order to experience that pain. But you don't want to experience that anymore now, so make a point of listing it as a new boundary.

It will also be necessary for your partner to spend some time on his or her own to make a list of his/her boundaries. Once you have both completed your lists, sit down and go through them one by one, still using the listen and reflect back approach. Where there is inherent conflict between your partner's boundaries and your own, you will have to agree to work out a compromise you both can live with. If you cannot find a compromise, then you may have to let the relationship go.

Probably the most significant boundary for most people is the issue of fidelity. When JoAnn and I went through our process, we agreed that our relationship would be a monogamous one and neither one of us would cross that boundary by having sex with other people. Had either one of us said up front we wanted to have sexual relations with others while in the relationship, that would probably have been a deal killer. Our friend made us discuss it fully to make sure we were clear on this issue. The advantage for us both is that we can be apart and yet have the kind of trust that can only come by having established this kind of clarity.

At the beginning of a relationship, this is not an easy issue to discuss and even more difficult to be honest about. Who would be brave enough to say to his/her fiancé, "I love you, but I want to be free to have sexual relations with others." But you can at least be honest with yourself. Are you the type who is polyamorous and will find it difficult to resist the chance to indulge in a little carnal pleasure on the side? If so, you really need to give it some thought. How would you feel if your partner did the same? Are you suited to be in a marriage or serious relationship that does not allow you to be your authentic self? It could be a deal killer.

We happen to have some very good friends who love each other dearly and are yet quite happy to support each other having extramarital relationships with other people if and when they happen to arise. They are totally open about their respective affairs with each other and still enjoy great sex together. They have a great marriage. But it only works because they are very clear with each other and support each other in being their authentic selves. As far as one can see, their relationship remains very strong and is not in any way threatened by each one having freedom to have other relationships.

When you have been in relationship with someone for a number of years and are going through the renegotiation process described here in this book, it might not be quite so difficult to discuss these kinds of issues. You can be more honest, open and frank because the likelihood is that you will be able to discuss it rationally based on how it has been for you both up to now. After all, you have a track record to go on and you know each other pretty well. Either one of you or both may have been tested and may have failed! (Is there still some forgiveness to do?) How do you want it to be going forward? What would you want from your partner? What are you willing to give up in order to accommodate your partner's needs? Here are some questions and phrases that might serve as discussion points in establishing boundaries and agreements.

> Commitment - What does that mean?
> Commitment to what?
> Intimacy - What does each of us need?
> Sex - Can we be honest about this?
> Fidelity - Are we of the same mind here?
> Flirting - Where is the line to be drawn?
> Freedom - from what? Freedom to do what?
> Honesty - No secrets
> Openness - No hiding our feelings

84

Equality - We matter equally
Support - Taking care of each other
Money Matters - Open and fair, equal shares, no secrets
Responsibilities - Understood and taken seriously
Decision Making - Joint
What's mine; what's yours?
Roles - Voluntary and enjoyed
Family Matters - Who comes first?
Children - Joint responsibility
Friends - Honor and respect each other's
Religion - Respect
Spirituality - Respect
Personal Growth - Support for
Alcohol
Smoking
Drugs

When you have your discussion, write everything down. When you have completed everything and have agreed them, both of you read out loud to each other the following statement.

"I promise myself that I will stand by my boundary statements and the principles underlying them, and I will not sell myself out. At the same time, I am willing to look at how my partner expresses his/her boundaries and will honor those too. Where they seemed to conflict, we have made compromises that satisfy us both. We are committed to going forward with this relationship on this basis.

Signed: _____ Date: _____

7. Breaking Up

Couples break up for many reasons; and in these days of serial marriages, a very high proportion of marriages fail. If the breakup has already occurred for you, then there is little I can say except to advise you to do the work we have already talked about. By that, I mean see the perfection in it all and do the Radical Forgiveness work to make sure the energy is cleared already, or is at least in the process of dissipating.

If the actual and final breakup occurred a long while ago and you are now ready to create a new relationship, I will address how to manifest a new one in Chapter 16.

In this chapter, however, I will make the assumption that you have gone through the reconciliation process, have tried renegotiating the relationship and have come to the realization that the relationship really is over. My goal then is to help you to see the process of breaking up as another opportunity to expand in Love.

This seems totally counter-intuitive, of course, because we are used to seeing divorces become bitterly contested fights over children, property and all sorts of other things, with both partners at each other's throats. This would be fine if you were still in the pre-awakened state and still trying to garner karmic units, but that is not what you want now.

If you are lucky enough to have a partner who is willing to work out an amicable settlement, for goodness sake, use a good mediator rather than lawyers, especially if there are issues which will survive the divorce like child visitation rights, property rights and so on. Lawyers aren't interested in reconciliation. Their orientation is towards creating division, the objective being one person destroying the other. [There are exceptions, like those who belong to the Holistic Lawyers Assn. and in "Lawyers as Peacemakers,"]

However, if your partner wants to make a fight over it and insists on using a lawyer, then you don't have much option but to do what you have to do. But again I say you can use the whole process to expand in Love. Here's how.

Preferably, well before legal proceedings begin and if you haven't already done so, begin doing the work to let go of any blame you may be holding towards yourself, your partner and any other person who might be involved in the breakup by doing the Radical Forgiveness work on the people you feel are responsible for it.

Write up as many Radical Forgiveness Worksheets as necessary until the pain subsides, as well as some Radical Self-Forgiveness Worksheets if you blame yourself for some aspects of the breakup. Use the 13 Steps audio processes as well in between. Doing this will have the effect of keeping your vibration high and, all the while, expanding in Love.

I would also very strongly suggest you do the Three Letters Process at least once if you have some anger and resentment to work through. (See Chapter 24.) That is a very powerful process and will result in your finding a lot more peace around the situation.

There is also an online program you might use to keep expanding into Love even while you release your anger or other emotions. It is called "Moving On," A 21-Day Program for Forgiving Your

Partner. The active part of this program puts you through an extended Radical Forgiveness program for 21 days. Each day, for those three weeks, you receive an e-mail and a task to do which will continue to move you into a place of forgiveness for your soon-to-be ex-partner.

[If this applies, check out the online program, by scanning here or go to www.colintipping.com/ online-programs.]

Hiring a Radical Living Coach might also be a good idea if you find you still feel in need of support to help you through the process.

As the process of separating and, finally, the divorce get under way, your challenge will be to maintain the higher Love vibration when everyone else is lowering theirs. That means doing your best at all times to see the perfection in every situation and refusing to participate in the (energetic) attack and defense game that is normally played.

I make the distinction here between the type of attack/defense played at the spiritual level for reasons known only to your soul and those necessarily hardball games you might need to play at the human level to get a settlement that works for you as well as your partner. I am certainly not advocating a passive stance when it comes to negotiating how things will be settled between you. You will need to be tough and willing to stand up for what you think is right (as opposed to trying to get everything you can and to hell with your partner), while at the same time maintaining a high vibration.

This is achieved by operating out of two parts of your mind at the same time. With your rational, mental and emotional intelligence, you stay present to what is happening and aware of how things are proceeding, taking care to protect your interests. At the same time, however, you stay connected to your Spiritual Intelligence which enables you to observe what is happening from the perspective of the bigger spiritual picture.

Keeping this awareness while standing in your own power enables you to stay in the Love vibration no matter what. This is not easy, especially if you are new to this, but you will be able to do it if you use the tools. Keep doing the Radical Acceptance Worksheets and the Radical Forgiveness Worksheets, and listen frequently to the 13 Steps to Radical Forgiveness.

Not only will this keep you expanding in Love, but the effect it will have on how things unfold will be quite amazing. Your partner will become more accommodating. His/her lawyer will become more reasonable and less confrontational. The judge will be more sympathetic to the issues. Your and your partner's families will be more supportive. Problems that seemed insurmountable will be taken care of and will seem to solve themselves automatically, and the eventual settlement will be a win/win for both parties.

This is explained already in terms of Sheldrake's morphogenetic field in which one person's energy can affect the whole field in quite dramatic ways, especially if that energy is Love. There is no stronger energy than Love, so its effect on the 'field' is very powerful.

But there is also another more spiritual explanation to account for how things tend to work out when you use these tools. That is, the worksheets and the other tools are a form of prayer. I call it secular prayer because it is not religious. It works just as well for atheists as for the most pious of people.

The tools connect us directly to our Spiritual Intelligence which, in turn, aligns us with Universal Intelligence (Spirit). The details get taken care of, and everything begins to work out. It's that simple.

Example: Jane was a well-educated, successful professional as well as a stay-at-home Mom before being sentenced to several months in jail for a string of DUIs. Besides losing her house, her divorce settlement, her car and her reputation, she also lost custody of her two children whom she adored. She was devastated.

When she left jail, she filed for bankruptcy and went into a residential recovery program. But her ex-husband made sure she would not get back custody of the children. Besides being an abusive, active alcoholic, he was a lawyer and used his knowledge and his vindictiveness to game the system against her in every way possible.

He made sure she was only able to see her children for 4 hours per week, supervised. Those visits were conditional on her paying about $1,500 a month to cover the cost of the attorneys, psychotherapists, custody evaluators and visitation supervisors she was forced to deal with. Her ex-husband would not pay for any of it even though he had lots of money. She did not.

This continued for a 1-½ years after her release from the residential recovery program. Each month, she would go to court with a long list of accomplishments and glowing references; and each month, there would be no change in the custody arrangements and no plan for future improvements. Her ex-husband had seen to that. This caused her excruciating pain, outrage and fear about her future with the children she adored, and she felt nothing but hatred for him.

She came to my workshop full of rage, frustration and a lot of shame. I allowed her to express her anger, fear and shame to the point of exhaustion and then had her do the spiritual reframe around the whole situation.

She came to the understanding that her children were not victims but, in her words, "angels of forgiveness standing by my side all along." She was able to see there was perfection for them in the situation and that she was never really separated from them in spirit. She got it that, in spite of how it seemed, nothing wrong had happened and that she too had not been a victim. Her ex-husband had not done things TO her but FOR her! With this realization, she was able to release her resentments and resistance to the whole situation.

A mediation meeting happened immediately afterwards during which her ex suddenly become very cooperative and uncharacteristically helpful. Things moved forward quickly and easily, and all the barriers to getting custody seemed to just melt away. All the officials suddenly became very helpful and supportive as did both families and everyone else involved.

Both she and her ex began co-parenting cooperatively without any professional mediation and have continued to do so ever since. Her relationship with her daughter is thriving in ways that would have been impossible had she held onto that resentment, fear and rage. She is able to help the children with their dad, in a loving way and co-parents with him and his wife without feeling any of the old resentments. Her drinking problem disappeared altogether; and at the time of writing, she remains free of that addiction. Life is good.

So this is how it works. As she expanded into Love by using the technology, the Universe responded, and everything worked out. This is why I call the workshop she attended "The Miracles Workshop." The results seem miraculous, but really they are not. It's simply the way the Universe arranges things when we ask.

PART TWO

THE AWAKENING

8. The Wake-Up Call

What usually precipitates the awakening is an experience that many people describe as being their 'dark night of the soul,' during or after which it becomes clear that, in spite of the fact that they have tried to make it as they would wish, their life is not working. They are exhausted and overwhelmed by their constant efforts to make things happen their way, and they are at the end of their rope. It feels like a total breakdown or burnout experience and is often accompanied by a series of lengthy bouts of crying and sobbing. Anger may be present too, but sadness and fear predominate. Suicide may be contemplated. There is a feeling of simply giving up. *What's the point? Why bother? Who cares?*

Did this happen to you? The breakdown experience might have been the result of some seemingly catastrophic event that acted as 'the straw that broke the camel's back.' Perhaps it was a divorce, a bankruptcy, an illness or an accident – some kind of serious pattern interrupt that precipitated a breakdown and changed everything.

Then, sometime after the breakdown event, did you have what I call a 'Satori' event? By this I mean something that caused an opening in your consciousness. It could have been reading a book like this one that did it, or something you chanced to hear on the radio. Perhaps you went to a lecture and heard something that caused a light bulb to come on in your mind. It is usually something totally unexpected and out of the blue. And maybe you couldn't help thinking that it wasn't an accident. I cannot tell you how many times people have told me that my Radical Forgiveness book literally fell off the shelf in front of them at the bookstore.

'Satori' is a Japanese word that means 'insight,' and it fairly accurately describes what was happening to you. Spirit was waking you up and saying to you, *"OK, you've done what you came in to do. You have as many karmic units as you said you wanted, so now you can wake up and begin the process of expanding into the true love."*

Spirit doesn't give the message that directly or that clearly, of course. At first, it is more a case of strange thoughts creeping into your consciousness, prompted by whatever your 'Satori' event was, like: *"Could the things I see as problems really be happening for a reason?"* *"Is it no accident that this happened?"* *"Is this all part of a bigger plan for me?"* *"Am I creating all this myself?"*

You also begin to notice a lot of synchronicities occurring that can't possibly be coincidental, and you may begin to feel you are being guided and in some way 'looked after.' You might get some past-life flashbacks or experience a number of epiphanies. Certain books may come into your hands that confirm what you have begun to feel intuitively. Certain people, too, might show up in your life in a way that is significant in that they have something to offer you just when you need it.

All of that is Spirit at work, and you are pulling it in through the part of your psyche known as your *Spiritual Intelligence.* That's the part of you that knows the truth of who you are, why you are here and what lessons you need to learn while you are here. It is the part of you that is connected to Universal Intelligence and is

96

helping to bring your awareness to a higher point and a more expanded Love.

As the process of awakening unfolds, everything suddenly starts to look different. For years, we had convinced ourselves that everything that happened to us was the result of bad luck, random chance and, in many instances, the consequence of other people and institutions intentionally or unintentionally hurting or damaging us by betraying us, abandoning us, cheating on us, lying to us, abusing us, discriminating against us, injuring us and so on.

[This is well described on a video that makes how we see life analogous to seeing either the front or back of a tapestry. Scan the QR code to view it or go to www.ExpandingInLove.com.]

When we were operating out of this kind of consciousness, at no point did it occur to us that there might be a divine purpose behind everything which was occurring in our lives. Our focus was on doing everything possible to avoid the circumstances that made life difficult, uncomfortable and painful. And if all of that still didn't satisfy us, we turned to alcohol, drugs, sex, food or computer games to dull the pain.

However, as we begin to realize that our lives might have meaning beyond mere accident and bad luck, we see that our so-called dramas are all part of a bigger plan. Suddenly they are more than merely the result of having married the wrong person, being part of a dysfunctional family, or having picked the wrong thing to invest in, etc. We begin to realize that all of these self-created experiences have had an important role to play in our soul's development. That allows us to become grateful for them all.

Those of you who have been through this process of awakening will agree with me, I'm sure, that this is a most exciting and exhilarating time, even if it is a little scary. After all, it takes a lot of courage to give up your victim stories, and many people have a lot of resistance to doing that. Some even balk at the prospect and go back into Victimland for a while. Many of their stories had been lifelong 'friends' and had served to create their identity. In many cases, they had used them, mostly in a totally unconscious way, to control others and get what they wanted. But as I mentioned earlier, what is even more scary about it for them is that they begin to ask themselves, "If I am not my story, who am I?"

Shift Happens

As you deepen into the awareness of the truth being revealed to you, a whole new opportunity to expand into Love opens up. You will begin to see the perfection in everything that has ever happened to you, it will become obvious that Love had always been flowing beneath every one of those circumstances you thought were so bad. As you come to recognize that things did not happen TO you, but FOR you, you will feel such gratitude for that Love, the Love of God shall we say. The more you realize that Love was always there and flowing through you, the more you are able to breathe it in and feel it filling you up. Others might call this energy the Universal Life Force, but it makes no difference what we call it. Whatever name we give it, it is essentially the Love that drives the Universe and breathes life into everything.

A Quick Meditation:
Take moment to breathe it in now. As you breathe deeply, take that Love in. Let it fill you up. Feel your heart opening and your capacity to feel love expanding. And then, as you breathe out, let that love flow out from within you towards someone you love, and let it be more beautiful and pure than it has ever been before. Do this for two minutes.

98

[To listen to me speaking this meditation, go to www.ExpandingInLove.com. or scan the QR code.]

Expanding Into Love

As you begin to let that Love fill you up, you will, with time and practice, come to have a lot of that same kind of Love to give out from within you. And unlike before, it will be a Love that is pure and authentic. It will be free of the need to judge and control because you will, from then on, always be seeing the perfection in people just the way they are and be able to accept them just the way they are. This is what it means to expand into Love. It is a Love that has the freedom to grow and to flower, even to the point where you actually become Love.

As I have already said, I am quite certain you would not be reading this book if you were not either at the beginning point of the awakening, having just experienced some kind of breakdown in your life, or quite a way into it. It might be interesting, however, to make a stab at estimating how far into the Awakening process you might actually be at this time in your life. How much have you expanded into Love? The questions provided below will help you make this assessment. Be honest in your assessment. It is not a matter of being more or less advanced than anyone else. Everyone is where they need to be. Any attachment to being in a particular position is simply Ego. Bear in mind, too, that although the Soul's Journey timeline (see page 9) suggests that the Awakening process is a linear process, the reality is likely to be a lot more complicated than that. I imagine it being a spiral process in which you keep going in and out of being awake.

I suggest you construct a timeline for yourself on a larger piece of paper or even a white board. Plot all your 'stories' along the time line prior to your awakening, as well as those during the awakening and beyond. The stories prior to the awakening lasted longer and had a lot more pain and suffering attached to them, while those afterward are short-lived and less pain attached to them because they are quickly reframed. It might look like this:

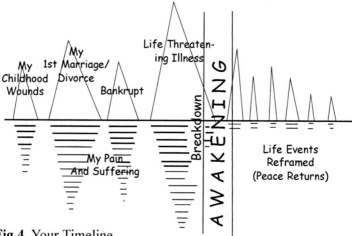

Fig 4. Your Timeline

Exercise:
It would be a good experience for you to answer and make some notes in your Journal, regarding the following questions:

1. What do you consider to have been your wake-up call, and when did it occur?

2. When, approximately, did you experience a breakdown or a dark night of the soul event that led to your Awakening?

3. What were the circumstances of the breakdown?

4. What book, seminar, workshop or experience do you consider was the turning point (Satori Event) for you, and when did that occur?

5. Who was very influential in bringing you to your Awakening (teacher, author, friend, etc)?

6. What was the nature of your Awakening process?
   - An instant epiphany?
   - A slow progressive change over time?
   - A dramatic and sudden shift in your world view of life as a result of a event?
   - A one-time spiritual experience?
   - A mental shift that later became spiritual in nature?
   - Other

7. If you feel that your awakening began some years prior to this time, answer the following questions to give you a sense of how it has changed you. Even though life continues to provide circumstances which are upsetting to you, how different is your response to such events? **DO YOU:**

   a) Stay in Victimland for a lot less time than before? *YES/NO.* If so, how much less in percentage terms? _____ %

   b) Find yourself being emotionally upset less than before? *YES/NO* If so, how much less in percentage terms? _____ %

   c) Stay present to your feelings where before you'd have stuffed them? *YES/NO.* If Yes, how much do you allow yourself to feel them no matter what they are: *95 -100%; 85 - 95%; 75 - 85%; 50 - 75%; Less.*

   d) Use the Radical Forgiveness tools? *YES/NO* If Yes, what percentage of the time? *95 -100%; 85 - 95%; 75 - 85%; 50 - 75%; Less*

101

8. In general, are you:

    a) Creating less drama than before? *YES/NO* If so, how much less in percentage terms?

    b) Finding yourself changing the priorities in your life? *YES/NO* If so, how are they changing?

    c) More understanding, tolerant, humble and merciful than before? *YES/NO* To what extent? _____ %

    d) Able to manifest more of what you want in your life? *YES/NO* To what extent? _____ %

9. Are you now aware of your life's purpose *YES/NO?* If so, what is it? Are you living it? If not, why not?

13 Steps to Radical Awakening

If you have joined the Radical Living Online Community and, therefore, have access to all the tools available to members, this would be a good moment to re-experience your awakening and expanding into Love by taking a moment to listen to the 13 Step Process to Radical Awakening.

[Go to www.radicalforgiveness.com/member or scan here to go directly the login page of the membership site to access the 13 Steps to Radical Awakening.]

As with all the tools, this 13 Step process starts out assuming that you are still thinking of yourself as a separate entity and then gradually leads you into experiencing yourself as an awakened person. Even if you feel you are awake, still go back to feeling separate at the beginning. (You may have to fake-it-till-you-make-it at first, but it works just the same.) Answer 'Yes' to every question whether you agree or not, and say it out loud if you can so your body gets the resonance of 'YES.')

9. A New Paradigm Emerges

As you awaken, a new paradigm of reality begins to fill your consciousness. As you deepen into it, you become aware that you are not just exchanging one paradigm for another but that you are living in two realities at the same time.

One paradigm represents the human reality while the other one relates to spiritual reality. While it certainly becomes clear that the human one is not as real as you thought, you realize nevertheless that it is exactly what you came here to experience; and for that, you begin to feel a sense of gratitude.

You also realize that each reality has its own set of laws which must be respected and followed. Since we are spiritual beings having a human experience, we must acknowledge and follow human law—or pay the consequences if we don't—irrespective of our knowledge that the laws which govern spiritual reality are more universal and much closer to the actual truth. While we operate in both realities at the same time, we have to be sure not to confuse the two.

All of a sudden, your life seems full of meaning and purpose. Whereas before, you might have been obsessed with creating security, money and a great number of material goods, your thoughts turn to more altruistic and meaningful goals, such as finding ways to be of service to people, being more mindful of how to take care of the Earth and all that lives upon it, and so on.

The extent to which you experience storge love rapidly expands and includes all of humanity and all living creatures, plant life and the Earth itself. Your compassion extends to the whole of creation, and you begin to feel driven to use your life in a way that will make a difference. Suddenly, money, status and image are not so important anymore.

It's not that life itself has changed. It continues on in much the same way and still provides its challenges. The difference is in how you now frame it as opposed to how you framed it before. As you awaken, you continually reframe your experience moment by moment.

Framing and Reframing
A painting without a frame is one thing. But as soon as you put a nice frame around it, something happens. The painting itself is transformed. Change the frame once more, and you change it again. The frame creates a context for the picture, and the two together become a unified whole.

So it has been with the story of your life thus far. It was framed in a particular way. Though you were not aware of it, you always were, as it turns out, the creator of your life—the painter of the picture so to speak. But you were also the one who framed it. With that frame, you gave your life meaning and a certain context by which it could be understood. Your frame is, or was, your world view.

In all of my online Radical Forgiveness programs, I ask people to look at six statements and tell them to evaluate which one or two most closely approximates their world view. How they score each one is a good indication of how they frame their lives, especially with regard to how their spiritual beliefs and ideas about forgiveness fit in the frame. It also shows whether they are in the awakening phase or not. I include them here for you to do the same thing.

Exercise
Score the world views on a scale of 1-100, with the one which is closest to your spiritual belief system being the highest, then down to the next closest. At least two of them are likely to be zero or thereabouts. Do the exercise twice; once for when you were still experiencing spiritual amnesia and then again for now, as an awakened human being. (If this is recent, you may not see much difference.)

Six World Views

1. I take a rather scientific/secular/rational view of life. I think that human beings are simply part of the evolutionary spiral and that like every other animal on the planet, we are born, we live, and then we die. Yes, there's a lot more to it than that, but that's more or less it in a nutshell. I am not a strong believer in a deity (God), though I wouldn't go so far as to call myself an atheist. I am not inclined to think there is a reality beyond what I register with my five senses. If there is, I have no real idea what that might be like. I am certainly not in touch with it and wouldn't know how to talk about it. Forgiveness to me means making a conscious decision to let bygones be bygones.

I think life can be understood and explained by science and by logical reasoning. The theory of evolution makes perfect sense to me, and that means life has no meaning beyond the idea that we have evolved from a primeval soup, more or less accidentally. My purpose in life has been to live it fully, earn good money, raise a family and make life as secure as

105

possible because life can be hard, relentless, chaotic and randomly organized. Life is just a string of random events that happen by chance, and I have to respond in the best way I know how.

Before ☐ After ☐

2. My spirituality and my world view come directly from my religious beliefs. I tend to see the world in terms of a continual struggle between good and evil. I believe that evil does exist, and it is my job to stay vigilant and defend against the ever-present danger of evil (Satan) coming into my life. God made this world, and He made me as well. He remains in heaven but is always watching and judging me harshly for having committed the original sin. When I die, I hope He will judge me kindly, though, and I will go to heaven. If I don't live a good life, I will go to hell. I believe in being kind to others, but I believe forgiveness is not ours to bestow. All we can do is ask God (Jesus) to do it on our behalf, so in my book, forgiveness is prayer and ultimately, should the prayer by answered, Grace.

I believe that life is a matter of following the laws laid down by God. I don't think science has the answers to life, and I think the answer to all my problems is prayer. I think my purpose on this planet is to be good, to be kind and to serve the Lord. Life is cruel and nasty, and suffering is the result of sin – a kind of punishment and a way of atonement.

Before ☐ After ☐

3. I am somewhat open to spiritual ideas and find them intellectually interesting, but I wouldn't necessarily call myself a very spiritual person. I am somewhat open to the idea that we come in to learn certain lessons, and I do try to interpret life this way; but I don't find it easy in practice. Even though I am quick to blame and see fault in others, I try to entertain the possibility that the person I am upset with is there to teach me something. I know I shouldn't try to figure out what the lesson is, but I am an intellectual person and love to know the how and why of things. I also get it at the intellectual level that the person is providing an opportunity to learn and grow, but I find it hard to really integrate that into my being. So I always struggle with that in real life. Again, I understand at the intellectual level that true forgiveness comes when we realize that everything happens for a reason, but in everyday life, find it difficult to put into practice.

I am still scientifically oriented and rational minded. I am skeptical of spiritual ideas though I am open to exploring them. My approach to life is practical, secular and very much grounded in an everyday reality. It is my duty to do what I can to make life meaningful and beneficial not just to myself but others too. I am concerned about the environment and social issues. Beyond that, life is about becoming educated, earning good money, raising a family and making life as secure as possible because life can be hard and unforgiving. Life is just a string of random events that give me the chance to learn about myself.

Before [ ] After [ ]

4. I see life as a mystery, not so much to be understood and figured out but to be experienced as fully as possible. I think the most spiritual people are the ones who are most human. I am very open to the idea that there is more than one reality. There is at least this physical reality that we inhabit bodily every day, but I am also very open to the idea that there is another reality that we cannot see which we might call the spiritual reality. I don't think anyone really knows what that reality is; but when I open my eyes fully and feel into my gut, I sense evidence enough that such a reality exists. And I am comfortable with that. I have my own way of connecting with that reality and expressing my spirituality (e.g. organized religion, being a member of like-minded groups, meditation, retreats, healing, praying, chanting, etc.); and I am happy with this. Forgiveness to me is done by extending compassion to the other person and seeing him or her as an imperfect human being just like me and everyone else.

I believe in angels, but I have my feet firmly on the ground and still have a hard time trusting life. I'm not sure what I believe, but I feel intuitively that life is more than just earning money, owning more things and raising a family.

Before [ ] After [ ]

5. I am a spiritual being having a human experience. By that, I mean that I have chosen to come to planet Earth in order to learn lessons and evolve spiritually. This is the school, and life is the curriculum. What happens during my life are my lessons. I have come into the life experience with the desire to fully grasp what oneness is by experiencing the opposite of it — separation. I had made agreements with souls prior to my incarnation that they would do things not so much to me, though it will feel that way while I am in a body, but FOR me. I also enroll others while I'm here to give me opportunities to learn. They look like my enemies, but I see them as my healing angels. That's how I see forgiveness — that everything that happens occurs for a spiritual purpose and that while we remain accountable for what we do in the human world, in purely spiritual terms, nothing wrong ever happens.

I am now aware of being in two realities simultaneously. I am still predominantly living in the world of humanity and feel very much grounded in the experience of being human; but at the same time, I am very much conscious of my connection to Spirit and have a strong sense of why I am here. I am comfortable with myself and am confident that life is supportive of me in general and is giving me lots of opportunities to learn and grow. Everything that happens is meant to happen the way it does for my soul's growth. There are no accidents. I use the Radical Forgiveness tools to release anything unlike love and Radical Manifestation tools to create the life I want. I am practicing the Radical Living lifestyle to the best of my ability.

Before [ ] After [ ]

6. I am totally into metaphysics, and I see myself now as a very spiritual person. One of the ways I see our life on this planet is being on the wheel of Karma, reincarnating over and over, lifetime after lifetime, learning lessons, balancing energies and evolving spiritually until one reaches completion. I am in touch with the spiritual realm and receive guidance from that side of the veil. I have several spirit guides, and I talk with angels a lot. I believe that we human beings are all part of the Godhead, the purpose for our lives being to assist God in expanding His/Her consciousness and, eventually, to co-create Heaven on Earth. As far as forgiveness is concerned, I am certain in my own mind that everything is in perfect Divine order and that there is nothing to forgive.

I am able to live in both realities at the same time and am grounded in both. I embrace life and know what my purpose is in living this lifetime. I am willing to feel my feelings fully whenever something upsetting occurs and then move through it quickly. I still use Radical Forgiveness worksheets to keep my energy field clear of things that might lower my vibration, such as resentment, jealousy, guilt and shame. I am willing to feel them but not to keep them. I can manifest what I need when I need it.

Before [   ]   After [   ]

Evaluation

I would imagine that World View #1 might have been you prior to the awakening, but since then, you may have moved on to at least #3 if the awakening was recent. If you scored high on #2, then I would assume you are still pretty much there. If you have been working on your life with such things as my Radical Forgiveness technology, Byron Katie's 'The Work,' Caroline Myss's 'Sacred Contracts,' Eckhart Tolle's *The Power of Now*, and other teachers like them, then you might have chosen numbers 4, 5 or 6.

Cultural Determinants

Obviously, since your world view is the sum total of all the ideas, attitudes, beliefs, preferences, values and prejudices that you hold about life in general, it has to have come from somewhere. Not only do you learn it from your parents; but the world view that you grow up with is constructed according to the values of the entire society you live in, including the religious institutions contained therein, even if you don't personally attend one. They still have an enormous input in how we all see the world.

For the reasons we have outlined, prior to our awakening, victim consciousness sits at the core of our world view. In this paradigm, the world of duality consists of victims and perpetrators, good

110

people and bad people, in-people and out-people. Whatever bad things happen, they are judged to be bad, wrong, unfortunate, unlucky, etc., and that it's right and natural to feel victimized, injured, wronged and damaged, probably by someone who should have known better. Justice demands that blame be apportioned and punishment meted out to anyone who betrays our trust, breaks the rules and commits crimes, etc. It is a fear-based paradigm that produces and even encourages conflict, competition, violence, war, discrimination, criminality, poverty, exploitation, cruelty and so on—all of which is Love but in heavy disguise.

As we have seen, this old paradigm provides countless opportunities to feel separation. However, the problem comes when you, having awakened, try to dump that old way of looking at things and begin living the Radical Living lifestyle. You were not the only one to have a stake in this paradigm. Society at large feels it has at least part ownership in it, so if you try to change it in any significant way, you will run into trouble. Others will hate you for changing it because change will represent a threat to their value system and their world view.

The best story I have by way of example of this dynamic involves a woman whose name is Patsy, who came to my first workshop in Melbourne, Australia in the year 2000. It was the first I had ever done in that country. Her victim story she came with on Friday night was that a few years previous, her then 12-year old daughter had been abducted out of her upstairs bedroom at around 2:00 a.m. and had never been heard of since. Also, just a few weeks prior to the workshop, her son had been killed by a hit and run driver. As you can imagine, she was in a very distraught condition when she arrived on Friday; but miraculously, by Sunday, she was completely peaceful about both events and was able to say, with impeccable honesty, *"I am at peace now, and I know from the core of my being that what has happened to my daughter is what her*

111

soul wanted, and furthermore, it is what my soul and my husband's soul chose to have in this lifetime as well. And the same thing regarding my son. It is all perfect."

To be honest, when she told her story on Friday, I felt unable to hold the perfection for her. I was almost ready to burn the book and give everyone their money back. But they said, "Let's carry on." So, I told them that they'd better realize they really didn't have a leader. So when it came to this outcome for Patsy on Sunday after having gone through the process of Radical Forgiveness, I and everyone else were amazed. What that taught me was that the process itself was so powerful that it worked, anyway— in spite of my and everyone else's doubt.

> *[The story gets personal for me at this point and I would like to share this with you on video. Scan the QR code or go to www.expandinginlove.com if you would like to hear it.]*

Anyway, the point of the story here is that shortly after the workshop, the police re-opened the case. She was interviewed again by the press, and she told them how she was now feeling about it. The press vilified her and painted her as a non-caring, hard-hearted mother who had no feeling. It was all over the papers for days. The police also treated her in a similar fashion. Even her own family disowned her. Despite that treatment, however, she held her ground and has never retreated into victim consciousness again since, which considering how badly treated she was by the public, is pretty amazing. Victimland is very seductive, and it's all too easy to be lured back there.

Exercise
In your journal, sketch out your own world view as you held it to be before your awakening, and then again after your awakening.

10. Picturing Spiritual Reality

Some people grasp concepts and ideas better if they come embedded in a story, so let me offer one that might illustrate the new paradigm better than a rational explanation. In 2003, I wrote a book called *A Radical Incarnation*. It was story about a soul named Jack, who was being prepared for his incarnation.

What follows is Jack's first person account of the initial phase of his preparation and the conversation between him and Harley, his Angel of Incarnation. You may find that it answers many of the questions you have at this time about the nature of spiritual reality, how we experience it at the human level and how it can be reframed.

"My application to incarnate had been accepted. I was to show up at the very next Incarnation Orientation meeting to receive my instructions. At last I would have the opportunity to be human — something I had been waiting for, seemingly for eons. Now it seemed that all my spiritual study and hard work had paid off.

To my surprise, I was to learn that for every one soul incarnating, there would be seven souls remaining on this side. No wonder there were so many souls in the room. An air of great expectancy filled the space. Because the room was circular, the seating was arranged in a circle so that all those seated could focus their LOVE on the beings standing on the circular platform of light at the center. Angels stood all around the periphery, singing softly in adoration and praise.

113

In a moment, one of the beings began calling out the names of those that would form each of the groups of eight souls. Once this was completed, we instantly came together in our groups. To my surprise, it became apparent that we were to vote on which soul out of the eight was to incarnate. As it turned out, I was the one selected.

Once this was decided, the next task was to come together with our incarnation angel to discuss the missions. I stress the plural because of a recent edict that had come down from above to the effect that incarnating souls would take on a whole lot more in their lifetimes than the souls who had incarnated before them. The reason for this, as it was explained to us, was that consciousness on planet Earth had shifted dramatically as a consequence of the Harmonic Convergence.

Apparently, this historic event occurred in the year 1987, and it marked a turning point in the evolution of human consciousness. The result has been the acceleration of man's developing awareness of TRUTH. Therefore, with evolution on fast-forward, incarnating souls are now able to take on many more assignments in one lifetime than ever before.

Our Angel of Incarnation was called Harley. He was an extremely old soul with great wisdom and a deep capacity to LOVE. He was a very senior angel, and I felt very honored that he was going to be the one to prepare me for my incarnation.

"It will look quite easy from up here," he said. "But once you get down there where the energy is really dense and heavy, it will seem very different. You will feel really heavy, and at times you will feel like you are trying to swim through molasses. Life will seem like a huge struggle.

"Whereas here in this world, your soul is limitless, when you enter the World of Humanity as an energy pattern vibrating at the frequency of potential physicality, it will become more bounded in the space-time continuum. As you go though the portal, it will have to squeeze itself into a much smaller human version of a soul with several different aspects. Some of these will continue to change throughout your human life while others will remain pretty constant.

"Once established, these factors will form the basic blueprint for your life. However, don't imagine that everything is set up in advance and that life is just a matter of fate. Or that we up here are controlling or micro-managing what you do down there.

"No, you are given complete free will to create your life as you see fit in the moment. You will be continually referencing your blueprint and acting from there, but exactly how you will do it will definitely be up to you. Deep down you will know your purpose for being in a human body. Exactly how you will choose to express it, (or choose not to express it, for that is an option, too), will again be up to you. You will know what lessons you have come in to learn, but how you will create them is definitely for you to decide."

I had to ask, "But Harley, what about the Divine Plan? Doesn't the term 'plan' mean that it is something fixed and unalterable? How can it be a plan if every aspect of it is subject to change by each individual soul? That sounds like a recipe for chaos to me."

"Yes, there is a Divine Plan;" Harley replied, "but it is continually unfolding in every moment and you are part of that unfoldment. Every action taken by every soul on the planet in every moment changes the Divine Plan for the next moment. Yet nothing gets out of balance. It is always in perfect alignment with what is called for just then. It all gets worked out in that moment. Everything is always perfect and at every moment expressing the consciousness of God, which of course is LOVE. That, in essence, is the Divine Plan. LOVE is all there is, and your part in this is simply to know yourself as LOVE."

"That's easy," I interrupted. "I already am LOVE."

"It's only easy when you are up here," he replied. "Yes, of course you know that you are LOVE. But the challenge for you when you

115

become human is that, for at least quite a large chunk of your life, you will not know this at all. All that you know about yourself as a spiritual being will be hidden — buried deep down in the unconscious part of your mind. You will not know who you are.

"However, the objective of the whole exercise is to rediscover it, to remember yourself and the truth of who you really are. At that point, you will be able to fully experience yourself as LOVE in a way that is not possible up here.

"You see, Jack, up here we can only know that we are LOVE. Down there, because we have a body with which to feel it, we can really experience ourselves as LOVE. That feeling experience is one of pure bliss.

"That's the fun part of the whole human experience. When, after experiencing the apparent difficulties inherent in living on the Earth plane, you begin to awaken to the fact that it is all really just an illusion, a trick of the mind and that LOVE **is** all there is, it will become for you a huge cosmic joke. You will have what is known down there as a 'breakthrough' or a 'realization' or a 'transformative experience.' You won't be able to stop smiling."

"But what if I don't awaken to this truth?" I asked. "What happens then? And how will I know to awaken at all if I am unconscious?"

"Many don't awaken," replied Harley. "And that's OK. They are still in service to others by co-creating all sorts of situations which, while they stay asleep, enable their co-creators to awaken to the truth. Remember, everything is perfect. They will awaken when the time is right.

"Besides your soul team up here, you will have a couple of guides along with you, sitting on your shoulder all the way through, guiding you towards that point of knowing whether or not to awaken. Both of them are aspects of your own soul; but in the process of your shrinking yourself down so as to fit the human version of the soul, they will become differentiated. They will certainly feel separate

116

from you even while carrying on a conversation with you from within. The first is the one known as your Ego. The second is your Higher Self."

Harley continued. "I will speak first about the Ego. It is probably the most fascinating of the two and certainly the least understood part of who you will become while in a human body. This aspect of yourself will be very instrumental in creating all of the many circumstances of your life that will constitute your learning opportunities.

"We will have very little control over your Ego from up here, except inasmuch as we have had to preprogram it to some extent to take you in certain predetermined directions consistent with your mission. But don't worry; your Ego is very creative and has a tremendous sense of humor. Combine this with a predilection for irony and a taste for the absurd, this guide is going to take you where you need to go, even if you have to go kicking and screaming! Its main role, of course, is to completely sell you on the idea that you are separate not only from every other human and animal species but from the Earth itself and, ultimately, from God.

"This guide will sell you on that long held and totally ridiculous idea that man made a decision to separate from God and that this decision was his undoing. It will persuade you that this caused God to get very angry. It is through this story that the Ego teaches you fear and guilt: fear that you have incurred the wrath of God and stand a good chance of being sent to Hell forever, and guilt for having committed that 'original sin.'

"In turn, in order to protect yourself from the fear and the guilt, the Ego teaches you how to repress those feelings and then, in order to get rid of them, to project them onto other people. This sets up a wonderful matrix of relationships between people who are not only in denial about themselves but who are continually projecting onto others and being projected upon. This obviously becomes fertile ground for the creation of many different kinds of learning opportunities. What a genius the Ego is!

"The Ego is also the specialist in helping you to become fully immersed in, and committed to, believing in all the illusions of the physical world. By that I mean not only separation but duality, right and wrong, good and bad, pain and suffering and, of course, death. Giving you a strong fear of death and the concomitant idea of total annihilation through death is the Ego's master stroke."

"Why would that be?" I asked.

"Well, if everyone knew that death was simply an illusion and that there was absolutely nothing in it to fear, people would keep choosing it just to escape the discomfort of the human existence. That would undermine the whole enterprise – which is, of course, to take on a body and be immersed in a world of separation and the opposite of LOVE so that you can go beyond just knowing that you are LOVE to the full experience of it – emotionally and physically as well as intellectually."

"If we want to experience ourselves as LOVE, why go to a place where so little of it exists?" I asked.

"That's exactly the point, Jack!" said Harley. "To fully become LOVE, you have to transcend everything that appears to be not LOVE. The human experience will throw at you everything that is not LOVE in order to test your ability to expand into that LOVE and, at the same time, expand the mind of God.

"I want to talk now about your other guide, the Higher Self. In the human world, there is always an alchemy of opposites; so it is perfectly in alignment with your human reality that there should be two guides who appear to be opposites.

"They will tend to always pull you in different directions. The Ego will pull you away from ONENESS while the Higher Self will always want to be reminding you of the truth of who you are. But that's their job. That's exactly what they are supposed to do for you.

"The Ego and the Higher Self are not, therefore, in competition with each other. They confer all the time and together, set things up for you to experience.

"From time to time, the Higher Self will lift the veil a little – just for a moment or two – to give you a glimpse of spiritual reality. There might be a number of reasons for this, but basically the Higher Self will do it to jump start a dramatic shift in your awareness – a process we call your awakening.

"But here's what you have to understand, Jack. We have set it up so that human beings can only experience that reality in a very limited way. We have given them five senses that can only work over a very limited frequency range, perceiving only physical realities.

"Viewed through these senses, the physical world looks so real that you can quite understand why human beings would believe that it is real and that there is nothing else. We have done a good job in that regard, but on the other hand, it has made the Higher Self's job quite difficult. It has all but cut people off from hearing its message at all, no matter how many subtle messages the Higher Self has tried to give.

"Fortunately, humans are now becoming more sensitive to the Higher Self and are becoming more open to the idea that their Higher Self is communicating all the time and giving them guidance. That is making things a whole lot easier and is speeding up the entire process which, as we shall see, is crucial.

"In the first three or four years of life, you will be intimately connected to your Higher Self and, in those tender years, may even be able to remember being here in this World of Spirit. As a young child, you exist quite comfortably in both worlds at the same time.

"But then, as the awareness of this world fades from your consciousness and the veil thickens, the Ego will begin to dominate. Your Higher Self will be in the background observing and guiding

where necessary, but it will mostly stay out of the Ego's way during the time that you are learning how to be completely separate and self-contained.

"Sounds like a whole lot of fun," I said looking around at my soul team. "Being briefed to this extent should make it a piece of cake."

"Except you won't remember a thing about it," said Harley.

"Spiritual amnesia is an absolute necessity. If you knew that all your experiences were simply setups, you wouldn't participate at the required emotional level. You would simply opt out of every one of them. The whole idea is to experience human existence as fully as possible and to go through it in the belief that it is real. That way, when you come back here, your awareness of ONENESS will be magnified many hundreds of times. Without total amnesia, this magnification would never occur."

"Then why are you telling me all this, and why do I have to attend all these lessons if I am to forget everything? That makes no sense at all!"

"Your education will come into play as you begin to gradually awaken and remember who you are. When your Higher Self begins to whisper to you, you will draw on these lessons from way down in your unconscious mind. Everything that I am telling you now will be down there, but you will have no awareness of it — at least until your Higher Self decides that the time is right to enlighten you about it.

"Let's talk about the issue of all this being purposeful in terms of the need that Universal Intelligence has to continue expanding its consciousness because it is central to everything.

"You've heard of the Big Bang theory, haven't you?" said Harley. "Humans have spent a long time developing this theory, and to tell you the truth, they are not far off the mark. The only bit they haven't yet fully understood is, of course, the most important part of the *whole thing. And that is the bit about what was prior to the Big Bang. Because they are so locked into the idea of time and space, they can't imagine anything coming into being without there being something before. It's a real problem for them. As you know from your previous studies, the material universe has continued to grow and expand. Scientists have actually measured the rate at which it is expanding. However, just as the material universe has continued to grow and expand, so has Universal Intelligence. God needs to continue expanding its consciousness in exactly the same way, for it too is part of that same expanding universe. You will notice that even on Earth, people talk about God as 'the Universe.' This is no accident.*

"Anyway, having unleashed the potential for infinite creativity, Universal Intelligence created us and all other intelligent life forms so it could continue its expansion. Indeed, that is the only reason Universal Intelligence created us."

"How so?"

"Since Universal Intelligence could not experience itself as itself, it created us so that it could continue to experience itself through us in ever expanding ways, in tune with the expanding universe. That is what is meant when we say that God is our Father and we are the son of God.

"Now, here's where it gets interesting," said Harley, leaning over to get closer to us as if he was about to share something of great value. "Without us, God isn't."

"I don't get it. What are you saying, Harley?" I said.

"It's really quite simple. God created us and gave us the ability to go in and out of that world of duality and physicality so it could experience that world vicariously through us. That way, Universal Intelligence would continue to expand in tune with the physical universe.

"We are vital to that expansion, Jack. Each and every soul who incarnates and all of those who, like your team here, support that process, are playing a vital role in expanding God's consciousness. That's what I mean when I say that without us, God isn't. Without you, Jack, God isn't."

"So, once I take on a human body, I am God in physical form playing in the physical realm. Is that right?"

"Yes," Harley confirmed. "It is as if the hand of God has put on a glove – and you are that glove. Without that glove, Universal Intelligence could not experience the physical world. What a gift you are to God, Jack."

"It certainly puts this whole thing into perspective," I ventured. "Wow, little old me helping to expand the mind of God!"

"Are you clear now why you are doing it and what it's all about?" said Harley. "Well, let me repeat it for you one more time — just to make sure.

"The basic aim of taking this human journey is to experience the opposite of what we know to be the truth up here – ONENESS and LOVE. Through the experience of those opposites, we can come to know ONENESS and LOVE more fully and through that awareness, move to a whole new level in our spiritual growth and expand even more the consciousness of Universal Intelligence. You also will recall that the human experience will set you up to be abandoned, rejected, betrayed, terrorized, and even tortured during your earth walk. Those are just some examples of things that will help you fully experience the opposites of LOVE and ONENESS. OK, Jack?"

"Well, I guess it's OK. Can't say I'm looking forward to all that though."

"Hey, don't imagine that life is only that," Harley warned. "A great deal of the human experience is totally wonderful and marvelous. There are many wonderful opportunities for people to experience

LOVE, bliss, harmony and peace in every day during their lives. But while they are experiencing the pain of separation, we like for these experiences to come fairly early in childhood. In this way, we set up a chain of unconsciously self-created repetitions of the same wound over and over again.

"For example, if a child feels it was abandoned in childhood, it will simply replay that same scenario over and over in all subsequent relationships. Similarly, the ideas that the child formed in response to that wound – like 'I am worthless, undeserving, unlovable, not OK, et cetera,' will be reinforced over and over again until it becomes the belief that drives his/her life. There will be so much pain attached to that toxic idea that it will drive some people to alcohol, drugs or some other addiction that they hope will medicate the pain.

"If everything goes according to plan, this negative belief will create so many blocks in their lives, they will, in the end, be forced to confront it and to heal it. And it is in the process of doing the healing work that the awakening occurs.

"Here's the point though. Who better to give you the initial experience of separation than your parents? The very act of being born is an act of separation, and for many people, the birth trauma alone is sufficient to set off the chain reaction. Other souls choose to have their learning experiences a little later, say at age five or six or in the early 'teen' years.

"Others choose to do it the other way around. They choose parents who will give them a 'nice' upbringing so they develop a false sense of security and then BAMM! The wake-up call comes when they least expect it.

"Good. Now let's get on with your preparation for the human life experience. Let's go and get your Divine blueprint," said Harley. "All the numerology has been coded in along with the astrological data, so it's all good to go. Then we'll program each of the chakras in the etheric-body field in order to establish the blueprint for the *physical body, which will, of course, only manifest the moment you incarnate."*

The Frame Is the Message
There was a lot in this story that might have been challenging for you and difficult to accept. Don't worry though. Remember the painting we talked about before. Each time you changed the frame, it automatically changed your perception of the picture, didn't it? It's like you couldn't help but see it differently. And yet you didn't need to think about it or have a belief about the frame itself, did you? It was simply a matter of whether it was there or not there, or replaced by a different frame.

No Belief Required
So, the fact is, belief is not necessary for the reframe to work or for the new paradigm to become real for you. In the case of Radical Forgiveness, which really is nothing more than the new paradigm in action, the new frame just needs to be there at least for the amount of time that it takes for you to register it even if only for a moment. It's enough, I believe, because it is, anyway, probably very close to the truth if not THE truth. It's just that our rational minds are not up to it yet. It simply cannot go there. But our *Spiritual Intelligence* is, and it registers the reframe immediately. So it sticks. That's why the strategy of faking-it-till-we-make-it actually works.

Love Your Own Humanness
But let's not forget that we are human beings with a prodigious capacity for making judgments, assessments and assumptions based on our need to be right; and we have an inbuilt urge to blame others for our unhappiness. This is all part of our need to be in victim consciousness in order to experience separation, but don't imagine that you won't feel the same once you have awakened.

You will feel the pain and anguish of what happens just as much as before; most likely you'll cursing and judging the heck out of the situation - perhaps even blaming people and making them wrong. The big difference, however, is how long you stay in that emotional state.

Whereas before you might have stayed in it for days, months or even years, you are likely to be through it in a matter of minutes. That's because your spiritual awareness of the perfection in the situation will break through the emotional haze and diffuse the energy. Your observer, the part of YOU that exists outside of you and observes you from above, will nudge you and remind you of who you are and how you are always creating your life moment by moment. That's your Spiritual Intelligence. All it asks of you is to love yourself for feeling what you were feeling and know that it is all part of the perfection of what is.

11. Soul Contracts

Part of the new paradigm is the idea that prior to your incarnation, you arranged with other souls to come in at certain times in your life to do things to you (actually *for* you), so you could experience a particular form of separation. For example, let's say that for the purpose of balancing karma from a previous life, you wanted to experience being betrayed. So you asked around in your soul group for a volunteer and found one who, for his/her own reasons, was willing to play that role for you at a particular time in your life.

Once you incarnated, you would have no recollection of this, of course, due to spiritual amnesia. During your life, you would have no clue that something would happen right on cue, exactly as pre-arranged. Let's say you had started a business which was going well. Your business partner seemed totally trustworthy, and it would never have occurred to you to check on her in all the 13 years she was with you. Suddenly you came into the office one day after having taken two weeks' vacation, only to find that she had emptied the account of all monies, including that of many clients, and had disappeared without a trace. As a consequence, you had to go bankrupt.

Understandably, you were furious and did everything you could to find her and bring her to justice and get revenge. The sense of betrayal by this woman was more than you could bear; and in the end, you went into severe depression. There had been many betrayals before but nothing on this scale. You went down fast, and you lost everything. This culminated in total breakdown and a steep descent into the dark night of your soul. (The rest of the story, you know.)

Many people are skeptical about this idea of soul contracts; but Robert Schwartz, in his book, *Your Soul's Plan,* offers some evidence which, while it may not qualify as solid scientific proof, is certainly highly suggestive that this might be true. After having a spiritual experience of his own that made him want to do this research, he gathered together one thousand stories from people who had been apparently victimized. He then sent some of these stories to various people who have the ability to see beyond the veil: psychics, mediums and channellers. He asked them to look for what might have precipitated these events.

When he got their respective readings back, there was an extraordinary degree of agreement within the group that each event had been the result of a soul contract which some of them described in some detail. One medium was actually able to hear the discussion within the soul group during which the agreement was made. Robert continues this research at this time and is writing another book. It is very interesting work, proving that a lot of pre-planning goes into how your life turns out and that what actually happens is exactly what we want to experience.

Exercise:
Looking back at your own experiences, which of them do you think might have been the result of a soul agreement? One of the ways of analyzing such events is to look to see what is odd

or peculiar about what happened. In the above story, for instance, it might have seemed so much out of character for the partner to have done what she did given her personality and value system etc., that it seemed absolutely incredible. If it was not her way to do something like that, was it her soul who did it in response to your request?

Another way to delve into this is to do a visualization. Imagine yourself as a soul who is planning to be born as a human being and you have around you a number of souls who are also planning a similar journey of their own. Now, think of someone in your human experience who you feel has previously victimized you in some way; and then imagine your pre-incarnation self asking one of the other souls if he or she will play the role of that perpetrator for you at a particular point in your human experience. He or she asks in return what will you need him or her to do for you. Your reply is what you used to think of as your victim story.

How does this feel? Do you have a queasy feeling in your stomach? Does it resonate?

Now imagine yourself agreeing, by way of return, to do something for one of the other souls in the group at some point during their lifetime experience. (You might think of someone you may have harmed in some way. Could this have been you playing out the soul contract for that person?)

Soul contracts can be of assistance to us in a number of ways. For example, one reason for asking a soul partner to come in and commit the crime of sexual abuse against us might be that we had ourselves been pedophiles in a previous life, and we wanted to balance that karmic energy out by experiencing being the victims this time.

129

There is also the need to enroll other souls in giving us the experiences of separation in order to support our mission. As I have pointed out before, I think it is highly likely that when we incarnate, we are given some sort of a mission to fulfill. We are seldom aware of it, of course, especially during the period of spiritual amnesia. (I didn't learn until I was in my fifties that mine was to bring Radical Forgiveness to the world.)

In my book, *Radical Forgiveness*, I advance the idea that Princess Diana's mission was to open the heart chakra of Britain by dying in the way she did after connecting at the heart level with the British people by sharing her wound publicly. It seemed very clear to me that she and Prince Charles had a soul contract to make that happen.

Returning to the story about Jack, the soul who was being prepared for his 'radical incarnation,' the plot thickens when Harley tells him what his mission might be. This will bring us closer to understanding the real meaning of expanding into Love.

> *"Sit down, Jack," Harley commanded in a soft but serious voice. "It's time for us to talk. I have something to tell you which quite frankly surprised the heck out of me when I got it relayed to me from Higher Command."*
>
> *"Tell me Harley — for God's sake!" I almost screamed. (Though I was really tense, I was not oblivious of the irony of having made my appeal for something that might make God happier.) "What am I going to be and do?"*
>
> *"Your mission is to become the President of the United States, heal the soul of America and then as a result of that — now get this — bring about world peace and the transformation of the human race. You will have the job of healing the shadow of America (slavery, betraying the native people, etc.) while at the same time bringing the world to point of breakdown so it*

can break through into a new consciousness somewhere around the date of 2012."

"Harley, you've got to be joking. I don't even understand what that means!" I was almost hysterical by now. "Why are you doing this to me, Harley? I just wanted an ordinary incarnation. This is way over the top for me!"

"OK, don't panic, Jack. It's all being worked out in advance. We've got a huge team of angels working on it; and you're going to have a completely different team assigned to you – all very old souls who will be able to support you every step of the way - so don't look so worried."

I was totally stunned, confused and afraid. "Why me?" I thought. "I don't want this kind of responsibility."

"There is also another soul who is being assigned right now to be the one playing opposite you in the drama that will unfold — the drama that will change everything. He will become a dictator in a country in the Middle East, and you and he will create a war that will precipitate the breakdown that needs to happen to bring about a particular and very much desired outcome."

"But Harley," I interjected. "Why me? There must be others far better qualified. What if I mess this up?"

"Jack, how many more times do I have to tell you that you cannot mess up? Spirit always finds a way. In any case, there is no one who has the 'right' experience because there is no precedent for this assignment. It has never come up before."

"What do you mean?" I asked.

"Well," Harley began thoughtfully. "You will recall that Universal Intelligence decided to expand its consciousness by first creating and then experiencing, through us, the three dimensional world of separation and physical form. Right?"

"Yes, that's as I understand it," I replied.

"Well, it simultaneously foresaw the time when humanity would actually awaken from the dream — even while in physical form."

"You mean that they would act there on Earth like we do here?" I ventured. "Like they would exist in a state of LOVE instead of fear, in complete harmony and bliss?"

"That's right," said Harley. "They would suddenly realize that separation was just an illusion and that there was no need to be afraid of anything, least of all each other."

"But, I am still confused, Harley," I said. "If, as you told me previously, the whole point of creating the illusion of separation was to magnify our appreciation of Oneness, why would you want to blow the illusion now?"

"Because that part is complete," he replied. "Enough souls have been through the experience on Earth to have magnified the awareness of the nature of Oneness, so the expansion of consciousness has been achieved. The need to create separation through wars, strife, hunger, discrimination, torture, abuse, pain and suffering is over."

"So why is it still continuing?" I asked. "Why doesn't UI just call a halt, declare it all one big fake, and bring everyone home?"

"Because Universal Intelligence is never one to rest up and stop expanding, and it doesn't want to miss an opportunity to expand in love even more by transforming a situation into something more wonderful. So, rather than just declare the game over, UI has set it up — and Jack, you're going to love this, it's so elegant — UI is literally planning to continue its experience of itself, as itself, but in physical form all the time!

132

That way it can continue to experience the bliss of existence as a FEELING as well as a KNOWING. Don't you see Jack? Universal Intelligence will create Heaven on Earth. Is that cool or what?"

"Let me see if I have this straight," I said. "Universal Intelligence has completed its phase of consciousness expansion whereby it created through us the illusion of separation and duality in the World of Humanity. But rather than just bring it to an end, UI wants to merge the two worlds together so that the vibration that we have in this world becomes the vibration of the World of Humanity as well. That way we can all have bodies whenever we want so that we can continue to have the benefit of being able to 'feel' as well as 'know' the bliss of Oneness. It is by merging the two worlds and keeping the benefits of both, that we can expand into Love and create Heaven on Earth. Do I have it right, Harley?"

"Pretty much so, I think." Harley replied. "There's a whole lot more to it than that, but that's a pretty good summation.

"However, Universal Intelligence never creates outcomes by decree although, as you know, it has the power to do anything It wants. It could create Heaven on Earth in a nanosecond if It wanted to. With Universal Intelligence, the name of the game is transformation which means that it's the process that counts.

"This is where you come in, Jack. Your role will be to set this whole transformational process in motion. As I have said, the light workers have been working hard making preparations; but the things that you do, the circumstances that get created as a result of what you do and the decisions you make will precipitate the collapse of the dream and cause a new reality to dawn.

"It might not happen during your actual lifetime, of course, since there are lots of stages to be gone through first to bring people to this new awareness. But then again, it might. You never

know. It depends on a great number of factors. It probably won't look pretty, though, because, since UI gave free will to every soul to enjoy during its incarnation, there will be millions of people who will put up enormous resistance to the change.

"They are so addicted to being victims that the idea of there being no right or wrong, no guilt, no blame, no anger, etc., will be just too threatening to them. They will group together and create a powerful mass Ego dead set against making the shift. They will use religion as a means of trying to maintain a reality based on separation and specialness, and there is a very strong likelihood that there will be many wars on the planet and a complete breakdown of the financial system caused by greed. This will all be part of the transformation process, of course; and if that's what it takes to break the illusion, that's what it will take."

Although it was published in 2003 (now no longer in print), the story turned out to be somewhat prophetic. As we all now know, a war did take place with George Bush and Saddam Hussein as the two main protagonists.

Fig. 5: Healing Angels

As I have already pointed out, you can tell if a soul contract is involved when everything about the situation seems really odd.

There was an awful lot about the Iraq war that was odd in the extreme. For instance, why did Saddam not stop the war by simply showing that he did not have weapons of mass destruction? Why did Bush insist on going to war with Iraq on the pretext of 9/11 when it clearly had nothing to do with 9/11? Why did Colin Powell, the Secretary of State, not stop the war by resigning when, clearly, he was against it? (It could not have proceeded without his being on board because he was the only one who had credibility in the world at large. Bush certainly did not.) Instead, Powell, against his own principles, went to the U.N. and gave patently wrong information in support of the war.

For these and other reasons, I think it is highly likely that there was a soul contract between Bush and Saddam to heal the world and shift humanity to a higher level of consciousness. I think it was Saddam's mission to become the world leader on whom America could project its shadow and self-hatred. His agreed role was to be the one to reflect the shadow of America and mirror it back so it could be transformed by Radical Forgiveness. Both souls agreed beforehand to play their respective roles as mortal enemies and agreed that the battle should be fought on the world stage in the form of a bloody war. By doing so, they would be serving all of humanity by bringing the shadow material, not just that of America but of the whole world, to the light for transformation by 2012.

Bush was projecting not only America's shadow on Saddam, but his own personal shadow as well. George Bush hated Saddam Hussein, and I have no doubt that Saddam felt the same way towards him. It was so personal for Bush that he even said that one of the reasons for going to war pre-emptively was that "he tried to kill my daddy." For a President to say something like that as a justification for war - that's another oddity!

135

The story was prophetic, too, in the sense that you have to admit that George Bush and his administration (almost) succeeded in bringing the country, and most of the world, to its knees just as he was leaving office in 2008. Could this have been the breakdown that was supposed to be followed by the break*through* into a new consciousness? He (and previous administrations, it has to be said), came close to achieving a worldwide financial and economic breakdown by giving the banking community free rein to commit fraud with impunity to feed their and the politician's greed (which is, by the way, part of the American shadow without a doubt), and in support of the American political ideology of zero regulation and an unfettered free market economy.

There being no impediment to their fraudulent activity, the banks indulged in selling worthless paper, all chopped up and rearranged into complex financial instruments that few people understood, which were not backed by anything of real value, including millions of mortgages they knew could never be repaid by the hapless borrowers. Through their greed and ruthlessness, the banks, in effect, 'killed' millions of Americans by cheating them out of their savings, their retirement and their houses. Saddam was also good at plundering the wealth of the Iraqi people and flaunted his greed by building lavish palaces all around the country purely for his personal use. Plenty of opportunity for mirroring there.

Then Obama came in and, together with the Feds, managed to stop the bleeding for a while. But at the time of writing the whole worldwide financial system is looking very shaky indeed and could easily break down in the not too distant future. If it does, then the world economy will very likely collapse, causing serious social unrest around the world and massive dislocation of normal living arrangements beyond anyone's capacity to comprehend or imagine.

I will come back to this scenario and how we might handle it in a later chapter. I mention it here only to illustrate how soul contracts can work at many different levels.

Another example for me occurred when I was giving a workshop in which there were a lot of Jewish people participating. As I was explaining the idea behind Radical Forgiveness (i.e. that everything that happens is all part of a divine plan and, therefore, perfect in the spiritual context), several of the participants kept shouting, "What about the holocaust; what about the holocaust?"

This is question I get a great deal in lectures and seminars, but my usual answer did not satisfy them. I usually say that such things cannot be explained, but if we find that Radical Forgiveness works in our own lives for less dramatic events, even though we don't know why, then we have to entertain the possibility that it must work for everything, including the holocaust - and other holocausts as well. (I was making the point that what happened to the Jews at the hands of the Nazis was not unique. There were plenty of other examples of genocide to be concerned about too.)

In the end, I got very tired of their constant heckling and interruptions, so I said this. "Look, what I will do if you are interested, I will stay behind after this weekend workshop and will present a three hour seminar about why I think the holocaust happened. You are invited to come if you would like to, but until then, be quiet about the holocaust. Is that a deal?"

They agreed, and 8 people turned up for the seminar. I really didn't quite know what I was going to say, but here's a brief summary of what came out of my mouth in that three hour period.

It seems to me that there is no race of people more committed to victim consciousness than the Jewish race, so much so that they keep on creating instances of victimization, generation after generation. I have demonstrated to you and you have found it to be true in your own lives during the timeline exercise, that we all tend to repeat instances of an original wound over and over again as a way to leverage the energy. We also saw that these instances tend to become bigger and bigger each time, until one is so magnified that it causes us to go into a state of complete breakdown. Also, we have seen that the breakdown is a necessary prelude to a breakthrough and the beginning of an awakening process. It was also suggested that souls agree to come into the life experience and do things to facilitate the breakdown and help with the healing process that follows. So, let's see if we can make up a story about what happened based on these assumptions.

I think it is likely that there are such things as group souls just like there is group consciousness amongst races, communities and even countries. So, on that assumption, I make it up that the group soul of the Jewish race decided that they had had enough of being victimized and wanted to put an end to the pattern they had established down the ages as their way of experiencing separation. The group soul knew it had far exceeded its need to experience separation; but since then, being victimized had become a very strong and powerful addiction that would be very hard to break. It knew that it needed a very strong loving soul with unlimited love and compassion to come along to help end their addiction to victim consciousness.

Spirit agreed to facilitate such a contract. Many candidates were interviewed until they came upon one they felt had enough love to do what needed to be done and, at the same time, would be able to withstand the hatred that would eventually be heaped upon him, not only during this lifetime but for many generations to come. The human identity they gave this soul was Adolph

138

Hitler. He would enter the human realm and would enroll another group soul that was suffering from its own particular addiction that needed to be broken. The German group soul.

Their addiction was their unbridled lust for worldly power and righteous domination over all others who were inferior to them, which was, of course, according to them, everyone else. Adolph would become one of them and, eventually, their charismatic leader. He would then immediately incite them to round up all the Jews, discredit them, humiliate them and gradually annihilate them in a dreadful and disgusting manner.

This was a perfect set up for the two soul groups. Led by Hitler, the Germans would create the worst possible form of victimization they could think of for the Jews so it would elevate their victim consciousness to such a great height that it would finally collapse once and for all and forever. The Jews' suffering would serve to reinforce the Germans' narcissism and self-righteous superiority complex until it too would implode under its own weight (and the bombing campaigns of the rest of the world), and collapse the energy that created it in the first place for a reason known only to Spirit. Those that died did so in service to their group soul, and each one of those deaths was a pre-planned contract and entirely voluntary. (Since death isn't real anyway, nobody died.)

So there you have it. That's my story of why the holocaust happened. It was a contract between two soul groups and one super soul with enough love to make it happen, the purpose being the healing of the two group minds. I don't know whether there is any truth to it, but I do know this. It is a better damn story than the one you have been hanging out in for generations."

The reaction was incredible. They loved it. The wife of the one who had been the most vocal and vociferous exclaimed she wanted to teach all Jewish kids this way of looking at things.

The discussion continued for a long time, and the question arose regarding the actual outcomes for each soul group. We agreed that the Jews finally got their own land and while they are still obsessed with security and always feeling threatened, they are supported by much of the world including America and most of Europe. At the same time, in the way they are treating the Palestinians, they are getting to experience the pain of being the perpetrators. So the healing continues. It's a long-term project for them.

The outcome of the war killed stone dead the German addiction to ideas of racial superiority and lust for world power. I have a feeling that the group soul itself died and was replaced by another group soul. I don't know, but it very much seemed that the German race had died and was immediately reborn. After the war, they did all they could to atone for the crimes they committed. Germany was also supported by the rest of the world and by America in particular to rebuild and renew their country. It was split in two for a while but has now healed the split, unifying East and West. Germany is now in the process of helping to support other states in the European Union get through some very difficult times.

[Note: Since having that conversation, I have had another insight about why these two groups chose to come together in a healing embrace. The German's claim that they were racially superior to anyone else on the planet was precisely mirrored by the Jews assertion they alone were God's chosen people and, therefore, spiritually superior to the rest of us. The holocaust was a way for that shadow material in the consciousness of both groups to get played out—and ultimately healed. It is still a work in progress.]

I Forgave Hitler:
One of my coaches, a Polish Jew, who is now in her eighties, having come to me at age 73 to be trained as a Tipping Method coach, experienced at the age of seven living and hiding in fear of her life just outside the walls of the Warsaw Ghetto. But she saw what happened within them. Had the Nazis found her and her mother, she would have been in there too, if not killed. She and her mother escaped by crawling many miles through the sewers. She passed out because of the stench, so her mother carried her most of the way.

After doing the training with me in America, she stated she had to go back to Poland to teach this awareness to 'her people.' She took a flat in Warsaw, and began talking to people about Radical Forgiveness. Her way of getting the attention of the Polish Jewish community was to say, "I witnessed, with my own eyes, the horror of the Warsaw Ghetto. I saw the kind of things a young girl of seven should never have to see. But I have totally forgiven Hitler. Do you want to know how?"

She invited my wife and me to go to Poland soon after that, and she had filled a theater to capacity – 350 people. 140 of them were enrolled in a workshop the following day. We then went on to Krakow and did the same thing. It worked because hers was a message of Love. Extraordinary Love. Extraordinary in the sense that the people who had been brutalized by Hitler were willing to imagine that his soul loved the Jews so much, he was willing to do what he did to free them from the bondage of their own addiction to victim consciousness. That's one heck of a 180 degree shift in consciousness for people who had suffered so much at the hands of Hitler and those he had hypnotized.

There are now more than 60 trained coaches in Poland and all my books are published in Polish. All this because of one lady's willingness to expand into the kind of Love that transcended all the suffering of her and her people. She has done seminars and workshops in Israel as well as in many other countries, spreading that Love even more widely. (There are also more than 100 trained coaches in Germany at this time.)

12. To Serve or Suffer

In my early 40s, just after immigrating to America, I had a reading from a psychic. One of the things I remember her saying was, "The choice is to serve or suffer." At the time, I had no idea what she meant, but somehow it made a big impression on me.

It was only when I began doing this work that the meaning became clear. In the context of this book, a reasonable translation might be that the choice is to "Expand in Love or Stay in Victimland."

Your Choice
As I mentioned earlier, even if you have awakened, you still have the choice to continue the process of growing and expanding in Love or to revert to the old habitual way of being. Most people choose to revert, if only temporarily.

I smoked for over 40 years. I quit many times, once for three years and again for two years, plus a lot of shorter periods of abstinence in between. Finally, I quit for good. The process of awakening happens in a similar way – back and forth, in and out until it becomes fully anchored in.

Peer Pressure
As we saw with Patsy's story in Chapter 9, victim consciousness is enormously seductive. The pressure to go back there is very

strong, and it will easily pull you back in. It's hard to resist because society at large, the media, your old friends and probably even your family (unless they have gone through the awakening experience themselves), exert enormous pressure on you to be as judgmental, critical and blaming of others as you were before. They want you to continue seeing the world through the lens of victim consciousness, not the new paradigm.

This used to bother me, and I would try to argue my case for being in the new paradigm. But I soon learned that if people are not ready to hear it, then it is a waste of time. I also realized that I was dishonoring them, and withholding love from myself, by assuming they needed to change and, by my seeing them in this way, was judging them to be less than perfect. How arrogant of me!

Everyone is exactly where they need to be. No one is lagging behind on their spiritual journey. No one is any less spiritual than anyone else. Everyone is on their own spiritual path, and each person's soul knows exactly what is right for them in this moment. There are no mistakes. Your job is to take care of you and do what you have to do.

So, my strategy now is to simply nod in agreement when people go on about how bad things are in the world, complain about the politicians, blame their spouses for their problems, etc. Why upset them? I quietly support them in feeling their feelings, because that is the whole point of the exercise – to feel the separation as an emotional experience – and I do my best to love them just the way they are.

This is not always easy for me. I have a tendency to be argumentative and, on occasion, I can't help trying to shift the conversation towards the other perspective. It rarely works, but occasionally I will see a shift occur; and every now and again, a light bulb or two goes on.

People who are sensitive to energy will pick up on my energy field and will feel a shift just by being in my presence. This is not to say I am special in any way other than it is a fact that people who have awakened and have committed themselves to the work of expanding into Love, vibrate at a higher frequency than those who have not. And people feel that. That's when they begin asking me questions about what I do. At that point, I have an opening. I also know that they too are at the point of awakening, or beyond it; otherwise they would not ask.

People are becoming more open and no longer think you are out of your mind if you talk about angels, spirits, chakras and energy, etc. Phrases like, 'there are no accidents,' 'everything happens for a reason,' etc., have become part of everyday language for most people today, so the mass consciousness is coming around. But when it comes to actually living those ideas and seeing the world through that lens, that's when they balk and victim consciousness prevails.

Resistance

Several years ago, I stumbled upon another reason why people resist going all the way into a full awakening. I was doing a workshop in Canada and had a room full of highly intelligent, spiritually advanced and completely awake individuals – or so I thought. As I broke through whatever victim stories they were still holding onto, in spite of all the work they had done in the past, they were sobbing almost uncontrollably, and all articulating the same underlying belief: "I'm not enough."

Now, since they were all highly accomplished people, I had to ask myself, for what were they not enough? For some of them, it was their parents; but even with these people, that didn't seem enough of a reason for them to be in a state of breakdown at this stage in their development. I suddenly realized that being 'not enough' is only a short step away from being 'not anything.' I began to see they were on the brink of becoming 'no thing.' One more step and they might lose themselves completely and merge into the Oneness – like the wave dissolving back into the ocean of consciousness – the ultimate act of expanding into Love.

To lose yourself and to die into the unknown is terrifying. What I was witnessing was their terror of going into that void. In coming to that place of 'not enoughness,' there was no way to go any further. It was either jump or pull back. They pulled back.

So, even if you are highly evolved, don't expect your victim consciousness to dissolve overnight. The higher your consciousness, and the more fear there is involved, the more you will come up against resistance.

My 40-year addiction to smoking was extremely hard to break. As I said before, I had tried many times over the years to do it 'cold turkey' and failed. I would pretend to have quit but would sneak out to have a cigarette, just cheating myself, until I was back on the 20 cigarette daily routine. If you were a smoker too, you can probably empathize with me on this. Even if you were not, you might be able to imagine what a struggle it was for me.

Real Addiction
But if you think that might have been hard, consider this. Victim consciousness is a 15,000 years long addiction! From the time when we were small wandering tribes to present day sophisticated societies, we have been dominating and controlling each other so much that we see no other way to divide ourselves other than into victims and perpetrators. No wonder we don't want to give it up! No wonder we go in and out of it even if we have gotten all the karmic units we need. No wonder the Jews didn't want to give up being victims. Small wonder, too, that just as I had snuck out to cheat and have my cigarette while claiming to everyone else I had quit (". . . as if they couldn't smell it on my breath – you idiot."

146

But then denial always makes us delusional . . .), we act and talk as if we were awake but actually remain committed to victim consciousness 99% of the time.

Denying the Pain
There are many ways to deny or avoid emotional pain or discomfort. Making a joke, especially a self-deprecating one, is one way to create a diversion and avoid the feelings.

We also force others to deny their pain in order to reduce the risk that we might feel our own. We do this by rescuing or caretaking. The most common way to do this is to put an arm around them or touch them in such a way as to signal, "Don't be upset. I am uncomfortable with you feeling your emotions." Co-dependents are often rescuers, as well.

Another way is to play the *'spiritual bypass'* game. Instead of allowing ourselves to feel the pain of separation, we immediately make some pseudo-spiritual comment like, "It was meant to be," or "It's perfect," simply as a way to cover the pain. The pain does not go away, however. Pain denied is pain repressed.

It's the same with positive thinking. We use it to avoid 'so-called' negative feelings by immediately denying them, making them wrong and replacing them with some (entirely false) positive feeling. Again, this is simply another form of denial.

In my opinion, there is no such thing as a negative feeling. Nor, come to that, is there such a thing as a positive feeling. They are just feelings, and they are there to be felt and expressed, no matter what they are. A feeling is only negative when it is repressed. Then it becomes toxic.

People are just as likely to repress or suppress their joy as their anger. The human journey that we agreed to take, as a way to feel the pain of separation, was always meant to be an emotional experience. That's why we agreed to take on a body, so we could feel everything. To the degree we won't allow ourselves to have our feelings is the extent to which we are denying our purpose for being here.

Ironically, though, it is a good thing for us to deny and repress our feelings during the period of spiritual amnesia. That way, we put some of that emotional energy in the bank so to speak, ready for the big breakdown experience. Then those repressed feelings will erupt like a volcano, giving the whole experience a lot more energy and power.

But once this has happened, and you have woken up, then it definitely is not helpful. A lot of spiritual people continue to do this out of habit, mainly by using the spiritual bypass technique; but the result is that it prevents them from expanding in Love. How can you expand in Love if you are not in touch with your own feelings?

Exercise:
Make notes in your Journal about your own strategies for avoiding feelings. Which of the following do you use?

1. Positive Thinking
2. Spiritual Bypass
3. Humor
4. Rescuing and caretaking.

13. Life Goes On Regardless

After the awakening, life naturally continues on just the same. It is every bit as likely to throw us a curve ball now as it was before. But now we respond in a completely different way. Most importantly, we begin to allow ourselves to have our feelings about whatever is happening and to be totally present to them. Depending on your self-evaluation at the end of the previous chapter, this may involve some extended practice.

You may well have to learn how not to suppress your feelings or deny them if that has been your habit for a long time. Bear in mind that you can't really expand into Love if you are not willing to open up to the full range of your feelings. The goal is to allow yourself to feel all your feelings no matter what they are. Here's a good 4-point rule that will help you become more in touch with your feelings.

1. Recognize the Feeling
See if you can put a name to what it is you are feeling. If you need help, consult the **Feelings Table** at the end of this chapter. But if you do not have it immediately at hand when going through a feeling experience, you can ask yourself this simple question: "Am I mad, sad, glad or afraid?" At least that will put you in the ball park of what you might be feeling.

149

2. Accept the Feeling

Be OK with the feeling and love yourself for having it. Do not judge it, especially if you would normally think of it as being 'bad' or negative. Again, there is no such thing as a negative feeling. It just is.

3. Delay the Expression of It

This may not always be necessary. If it is anger or something similar, and if you were to express it in the moment and it would cause problems, delay expressing it until it is safe to do so. But don't use this as an excuse for not ever expressing it though.

4. Express the Feeling

Find a way to let the feelings come out through speaking it out, crying, shouting, beating cushions or whatever way you can that is safe. You might need to do it with someone who can support you in doing this.

Emotions:

Notice that up to now, I have been talking about feelings - not emotions. A feeling is something that happens in the body. It is not an emotion until there is a thought attached to it.

The definition of an emotion, therefore, is *"A thought attached to a feeling."* Which comes first, the thought or the feeling? I don't know, but clearly the thought is a mental thing while the feeling is physical; and the two necessarily go together.

However, while the feeling component is a totally physical phenomenon and not under our direct control, we do have dominion over our conscious thoughts. That means if we change our thought process, we automatically have an effect on the feeling. In other words, it becomes a different emotional experience.

So, here's what's so interesting about this. Prior to the awakening, when something disturbing happens, we seize the opportunity to leverage the pain by *'awfulizing' it*. That is to say we increase the emotional quotient of the event by using adjectives like awful, terrible, tragic, untimely (as in early death), disgusting, disastrous, criminal, wicked and so on; and we go around hysterically shouting for revenge on whomever might be to blame. It can extend the whole painful experience for months and sometimes even years. This shows how we use our thoughts to magnify our feelings and enlarge the event itself.

Once we understand the game and realize that whatever is occurring is happening for a reason, even if we can't see what it is, our response is completely different. Even though we are free of the need to magnify the pain, we certainly allow ourselves to have the normal emotional response to whatever is occurring. We are bound to; we are human beings.

But now, instead of awfulizing it with thoughts that expand the pain both in time and intensity, we bring thoughts of perfection, peace and love to the situation. This has the effect of diminishing our pain and altering our perception of the drama surrounding it.

This is very different to doing a spiritual bypass, however. When we do that, we use the words in a superficial way as a way to avoid feeling even those raw, non-awfulized feelings we naturally would have in such a situation. It is a defensive move based in fear and, as such, weakens our ability to take action. It is disempowering.

Making a conscious decision to have an awareness of the Love that is flowing beneath the seemingly disastrous situation, on the other hand, is empowering because it brings us to a place where we can tap into the power of peace and Love. When we do this, we are empowered (with guidance from above) to act quickly in doing whatever needs to be done to help the situation. This enables us to have complete focus on the job at hand. Holding in our consciousness that it was somehow perfect in the spiritual sense enables us to move through the feelings very quickly. We can be of much greater assistance in the situation than those who are immobilized as a result of having either awfulized it or denied it.

This is why we have developed a strategy specifically to help us deal with large world events over which we have little control but which we can transform energetically if we apply the Radical Forgiveness technology to them. (See the Radical Transformation Strategy in Chapter 14: Radical Living.)

Having said this, I want to make it clear that I am not making the case for affirmations. They don't work, and the reason is that for every affirmation we make with our conscious mind, the subconscious mind will have an opposing one that is a hundred times more powerful. The subconscious mind will always override whatever is presented by the conscious mind if it feels inclined to do so because it has infinitely more power.

The subconscious mind operates on a binary system. It's always either/or. Pain or pleasure; true or false; known or unknown; right or wrong; good or bad. It does not think or rationalize. It simply works by trying to find a match between what is presented by the conscious mind and its own data bank composed of beliefs, memories, established ideas, opinions and prejudices. If my conscious thought (affirmation) doesn't fit what is already in the data base, it will reject it, no matter how rational it is or how much we want it.

That's exactly why I couldn't stop smoking. Giving up cigarettes was a rational choice. I knew they were unhealthy and might cause lung cancer, but my subconscious mind was addicted to the pleasure they gave me; so my sensible rational choice was always overridden. Eventually I did quit but only by using hypnosis to put my subconscious mind in park for a while.

Bearing in mind that the subconscious mind is pre-programmed, not only by your parents and society in general but reinforced by 15,000 years of victim consciousness, generation after generation, what chance do you think a stated affirmation has against such programming? Nil. I don't care how many 'Post-its' you arrange on your mirror at home or how many 3" x 5" cards you keep in your car to look at when you get in. If the affirmation is not in complete agreement with what is down in the subconscious mind, nothing will change.

My approach to making change permanent does not rely on trying to reprogram the subconscious mind at all. What I do is teach people how to use tools that skip around the subconscious mind altogether, allowing them to simply access their *Spiritual Intelligence* instead.

This system has become known as *The Tipping Method* and has become the basis for a number of Strategies for Radical Living, including Radical Forgiveness, Radical Manifestation, Radical Health, Radical Grieving and Radical Reconciliation. These are briefly explained in Chapter 14; but now, having mentioned Spiritual Intelligence, I should make the distinction between this and the other two types of intelligence - mental and emotional.

Mental Intelligence is the intelligence of the mind. We are all familiar with it and know how to measure it accurately. It covers all cognitive activity of the rational mind – thoughts, ideas, concepts, paradigms, theories. It is a highly developed faculty in humans even though it varies a lot between individuals. It has enabled us to go to the moon and back, develop amazing medical procedures to cure disease, and to develop sophisticated models of the world through science and mathematics, among millions of other wonderful achievements that have benefitted mankind.

Emotional Intelligence is the intelligence of the heart. It handles our emotional responses to the life experience and helps us to sort out what thoughts are attached to the feelings. It guides our emotional responses to life – whether fear-driven, love-driven, guilt-driven, pleasure-driven, etc. It tells us when we are in denial, lying and out of integrity. It enables us to relate to each other at the heart level with compassion, empathy, tolerance, humility, forgiveness, etc. Without emotional intelligence, we would either be like robots – machines that can think but can't feel, or sociopaths unable to control our emotions.

Even though emotional intelligence has great wisdom, people are taught to value mental intelligence more and to deny their feelings. Consequently, emotional intelligence is quite suppressed in humans. Even so, the power of our raw, unchecked emotions to override our mental intelligence – especially in the subconscious parts of the mind – is strong. The result is the formation of negative mental structures like bigotry, prejudice, unreasonable attitudes, inflexibility of mind, false beliefs, denial and so on. All of these fit in perfectly with victim consciousness but have no place in someone who has awakened and is exploring the notion of Oneness.

Spiritual Intelligence is the intelligence of the Higher Self. It is the most subtle of the three and operates below our level of awareness. It knows the truth of who we are, and it connects us to the world of Spirit and Universal Intelligence (God). Our body is the antennae for our Spiritual Intelligence. Our Spiritual Intelligence guides us on our spiritual journey, always moving us in the direction of growth and healing. It is our internal spiritual compass. It keeps us on track with our Divine Plan. It finds its outer expression in our everyday lives as religious or spiritual practice, the search for meaning beyond this reality, contemplation

154

and meditation, prayer, etc. It is not bound by time and space. It comes into play when we ask for help and open up to receiving help from the spiritual realm. The tools and processes associated with the Radical Living approach provide a perfect way to ask for help, even if we are skeptical about the whole idea.

The tools mentioned above which activate our Spiritual Intelligence do not, of course, come into play until we have come through the breakdown experience and have awakened enough to be ready to begin the work. Once we have dissolved all the old energies associated with everything we created previously, then they can support us in staying awake and moving forward with conscious awareness. That's what they do.

Finally, in the light of all this, let me come back to the issue of the difference between doing a spiritual bypass and shifting your awareness to the Love that is flowing beneath any given unpleasant situation. When we employ spiritual language in the spiritual bypass, we are using our mentality. This only creates denial. When we shift our thinking towards the Love vibration, we are using our Spiritual Intelligence to shift the energy. This creates a totally different order of effectiveness. Not only does using our Spiritual Intelligence change how we feel personally, but it often causes the situation itself to change for the better.

The Feelings Reference Table
Some people have difficulty identifying their feelings, especially men. The following table is designed to help us find words that describe how we might be feeling and builds on the basic list of being either mad, sad, glad or afraid.

FEELINGS CHECK

MAD	SAD	GLAD	AFRAID	PEACEFUL	POWERFUL
Withdrawn	Remorseful	Amused	Overwhelmed	Responsive	Appreciated
Irritated	Stupid	Optimistic	Co-dependent	Nurturing	Independent
Betrayed	Isolated	Playful	Submissive	Confident	Respected
Abandoned	Apathetic	Stimulated	Bewildered	Thoughtful	Grounded
Hurt	Empty	Amusing	Embarrased	Thankful	Valued
Frustrated	Depressed	Excited	Controlling	Content	Deserving
Resentful	Ashamed	Energized	Inadequate	Trusting	Engaged
Hostile	Hopeless	Fascinated	Dependent	Tolerant	Confident
Angry	Rejected	Fascinating	Confused	Relaxed	Humble
Hateful	Guilty	Daring	Helpless	Loving	Worthy
Critical	Lonely	Cheerful	Anxious	Present	Strong
Jealous	Beaten	Hopeful	Insecure	Serene	Secure
Vengeful	Tearful	Creative	Absent	Alive	Proud
Rageful	Bored	Happy	Alone	Full	Able

Fig. 6: Feelings Reference Table

PART THREE

RADICAL LIVING

14. Radical Living

Even though we may have embraced the new paradigm for ourselves, life goes on much the same. The world we live in at the time of writing is still committed to the old paradigm, at least for now. And just because we've woken up doesn't mean that we don't still have a lot to learn and challenges to face.

But in order for each one of us to stay awake, we need to develop a habit of mind and a corresponding lifestyle that always defaults to the new paradigm. I call this the Radical Living lifestyle.

Yet, given where we are in terms of our consciousness, we still need a lot of help in living this way and being true to ourselves. This is why we have developed a number of strategies that help us to develop the Radical Living lifestyle. They are all extensions and adaptations of the same tried and true 'technology' of Radical Forgiveness, with all its tools and processes, that has proven so effective over the years. This is why it is Strategy #1.

Strategy #1: Radical Forgiveness
Weaning yourself away from victimhood is really the first step in developing a Radical Living consciousness. You cannot be in a peaceful state if you are holding resentment and anger about things that have happened in the past or continue to rob you of your peace

even now. It is incredibly disempowering to make others responsible for your lack of happiness. When you do Radical Forgiveness, you take back your power.

Strategy #2: Radical Empowerment

This strategy includes both self-forgiveness and self-acceptance and can be defined as 'the art of accepting the consequences of being yourself.' While it can be said that all forgiveness is self-forgiveness and for that reason don't need a separate strategy for self-forgiveness and self-acceptance, we still seem to need a strategy that helps us escape the tyranny of the inner critic and inner judge. Both conspire to disempower us and make us feel unworthy and flawed. But more than that, we can't develop a Radical Living consciousness if we are not willing to see, even in circumstances where our guilt is appropriate and our shame justified, that there must have been some spiritual reason why we were 'called' to do what we did and that from the spiritual big picture standpoint, we made no mistake.

Strategy #3: Radical Transformation

We need this strategy to help us to fake-it-till-we-make-it and to use our own Spiritual Intelligence to connect into the higher truth of what appears to be happening out there in the world that seem so bad, like wars, famine and natural disasters. The tools it provides help us maintain our willingness to entertain the possibility (notice I don't say believe) that such events are all part of a divine plan, while at the same time feeling compassion and empathy with and for the people involved and being motivated to take action to help alleviate the suffering. When we do take action while holding this perspective, we are much more powerful because we are doing it with a consciousness that is free of the need to blame or add to the pain by getting angry and upset. If we remain willing to see the hand of God in the situation, we will, simply by virtue of our vibration, be of much greater help to those who are hurting than we otherwise would.

160

Many people who consider themselves spiritual make a virtue out of avoiding the news on the grounds that it is too negative. I have some sympathy with that idea if only because the news can be so distorted, but the fact is that reported events are only negative (and therefore toxic) if we remain blocked off from the idea that there is a spiritual purpose being served by them.

In fact, it can be very good spiritual practice, from a Radical Living point of view, to make a point of exposing oneself to the pain and suffering of, say, earthquake victims or a mass shooting or some other awful event, and doing one's best to remain open to seeing the perfection in the situation. That's why I would recommend you keep the Radical Transformation Worksheets handy and use them when you see something on the news that is really upsetting. I also suggest that having the 4-Steps Emerge-n-See process in your mind will also be very helpful. (This process is explained in detail later in this chapter.)

This not only helps you keep your vibration high, but I feel certain that it helps raise the collective consciousness as well. It also contributes to the improvement of the actual situation itself in a profound way. Even while you sit in your armchair watching events unfold on the other side of the world perhaps, you will be making difference if you hold it that there is perfection in the situation.

Strategy #4: Radical Manifestation

This strategy empowers you to use the Law of Attraction effectively to create the things and situations that you desire to have in your life, such as a new relationship, the baby you've always wanted, a job or new career, the kind of house you want, and so on. In more general terms, it is about creating the kind of life that will be meaningful and fulfilling to you as someone who has awakened and wants to make a difference. As I pointed out earlier, when someone goes through the dark night of the soul and emerges as an awakened person, their priorities change. Whereas before, you

161

might have been very fixated on material things that made you feel in control, safe, prosperous and successful, your focus shifts to making a difference and being of service to humanity, the environment and the community. Having used Radical Forgiveness and Radical Self-Forgiveness to retrieve your energy from the past, you now have more energy in present time to create the future you envision for your new life. This you do by using the strategy of Radical Manifestation.

Strategy #5: Radical Relationships
In this strategy, we use a combination of Radical Forgiveness, Radical Self-Empowerment and Radical Manifestation to create the relationships we want. A lot of this strategy has been covered already in this book, with more to come in Chapter 16 about manifesting a new relationship.

Strategy #6: Radical Money
Most of our beliefs, prejudices and attitudes are rooted in the old paradigm, which is why we have such a hard time dealing with money. We cannot truly live a Radical Living lifestyle if we are not willing to accept that the Universe is infinitely benevolent and a place of total abundance. We have developed a number of worksheets and sophisticated online programs to help people change their consciousness around money so they can magnetize, and feel more comfortable with attracting more money than they are used to having.

[Even though it is counted as a strategy here, money consciousness is not covered in this book. For more on this topic and to learn about the online program that is designed to increase your income, scan the QR code to go to www.colintipping.com/ online-programs.]

Strategy #7: Radical Weight Loss

"The Only Things You Have to Give Up With This Program Are the Stories That Caused You to Put the Weight On In the First Place." That's the tag line for the online weight loss product associated with this strategy. We developed this one when it became clear that one of the side effects of doing a Radical Forgiveness workshop was that people who were carrying a lot of excess fat automatically lost weight. The fat was serving a function associated with their stories. Once they let go of their stories, the fat was able to go too. This is now offered as an online program.

[For the details of the Radical Weight Loss Program go to www.colintipping.com/online-programs or scan the QR Code.]

Strategy #8: Radical Reconciliation

Whereas forgiveness is done only by the person forgiving, reconciliation requires reciprocity. Both parties need to have a desire to come together and reconcile their differences. Members of the Radical Living Online Community will find a comprehensive Radical Reconciliation Worksheet that, while the assumptions of the new paradigm are embedded in it, becomes a very practical tool to help people have a meaningful dialogue about how they might come together and find common ground.

Strategy #9: Radical Grieving

This strategy is covered in great depth in Chapter 26, but briefly the goal is to help those who have suffered a loss to reduce their pain by applying some of the assumptions of the new paradigm to the situation.

In short, these strategies and the tools they each offer simply provide a way to ask for help. For example:

"Help me truly forgive myself and others."

"Help me see my projections and my judgments."

"Help me love this part of myself."
"Help me deepen my ability to love."
"Help me create what I need."
"Help me see the true meaning of life and death."
"Help me find my purpose,"
"Help me see the truth of what is, as is."
. . .and so on.

We need the tools that each strategy provides because the Radical Living approach is a hard road to follow. First and foremost, it requires trust. To be an awakened person, we need to believe that we are always being taken care of and will be given the guidance we need. It takes a lot of courage to live that way; but the more we are willing to take the risk of being true to ourselves, the more protected and guided we will become. It takes a lot of humility to be awakened because the more conscious we become, the more we realize how little we know and how little we control. Willingness to surrender to what is, as is, turns out to be the key to Radical Living.

Our lessons are, in many ways, harder to learn because we can't hide any more. For example, when living the Radical Living lifestyle, we can't shift the blame for our shortcomings onto other people. That's because we know that we are solely responsible for our lives and we create our lives moment by moment. As an awakened person, we now see every person about whom we have judgments as reflecting what we hate in ourselves and have projected onto them – parts of ourselves we need to love.

If we are to live this way and really expand in Love, we must begin to surrender to what is and accept things as they are, even if they seem intolerable. Rather than attending to what others tell us, if we listen to our inner guidance and let it be our true compass we will be led to do what is right.

Avoiding Victimland
As we have seen, if we are not fully anchored in the new paradigm, there is always the likelihood of being seduced back into a victim's frame of mind. To reduce that likelihood, let me introduce a Radical Living tool to use in the moment something upsetting occurs, which will save you many a trip to Victimland – something which is to be avoided at all costs.

If you go back there, you immediately go unconscious again. Spiritual amnesia returns, so you are stuck there for a long time without really knowing it. It's like an alcoholic who has been sober for a year and takes one drink. He's down again and back where he started. It's the same with you if you go to Victimland. The old addiction to victim consciousness takes over, and you forget everything about the new paradigm. You may be stuck there for a long time unless you have someone who can get you out of there. (This is why you need a Radical Living support group; more about this later.)

The Emerge-n-See, 4-Step Process
This is the tool I mentioned earlier under Strategy # 3. It is actually part of the Radical Forgiveness Strategy about which I will say a lot more in later chapters, but I want to mention the process now since it is the one tool you will continue to use on a very regular basis while developing your Radical Living habit. It is the tool we recommend you use to avoid the Victimland trap. Its continued use, in conjunction with other tools, will enable you to finally break the addiction to victim consciousness.

The following three articles from my regular newsletter were written immediately after doing a training for business people in Switzerland in June 2011, in which they had fed back to me how useful this tool had become in keeping their business free from difficulties. I think you will find these articles instructive, as written, about how valuable a tool this 4-Step Process might be.

Article #1. The Wisdom of Simplicity

*Once again, while teaching a class in Switzerland, I was shown that **less is more**. I don't normally get the chance to teach the same group of people twice, which means I seldom ever get feedback from an entire group. But on this occasion, I was teaching the second of three consecutive weekend training sessions called 'Spirituality in Business,' for the same group of 20 business people. Their feedback from their first session surprised me.*

*During that first session I had them experience the Radical Forgiveness tools. I told them to use them between then and their next session and to report on how useful they had been – if at all. They reported great results with the RF Worksheet and the 13 Steps; but almost unanimously said the most useful tool, and the one they came to rely on the most, especially in the work context, was the **"Emerge-n-See" 4-Step Process**. What they liked about it was that it was very quick, could be used in the instant something happened, and it transformed the energy immediately. And it was easy to memorize, so they didn't have to go find a worksheet or play a CD.*

I have to admit that up to now, I have tended to emphasize the Radical Forgiveness Worksheet and the 13 Steps CD, and then to mention the 4-Steps almost as an afterthought. However, if a group of business owners, managers and entrepreneurs found the 4-Steps to be far and away the most useful tool, even after having had only a weekend introduction to Radical Forgiveness and how it might be used in the workplace, then clearly I have to take notice and to let you know about this development, that is if you haven't discovered this for yourself already.

It may well be symptomatic of the general speed-up in the rate at which consciousness is shifting and evolving. Just as we no longer need gurus to follow like we did in the 60s and 70s, perhaps we now are reaching the point where we need only the simplest of tools to remind us of the truth that lies within and is now easily accessed. There's no doubt that the entire philosophy of Radical Forgiveness is contained in those four steps, as well as the reminder to choose peace and resist the urge to blame and feel victimized. You simply say these to yourself whenever something 'bad' happens. Let me remind you what they are:

1. Look What I Created!
(Accepting that you are the creator of all circumstances in your life, and that there is a purpose in all that is happening.)

2. I Notice My Judgments and Feelings But Love Myself Anyway.
(Acknowledging your humanness and being aware of your feelings, judgments and thoughts.)

3. I Am Willing to See the Perfection in the Situation.
(The Radical Forgiveness step.)

4. I Choose Peace.
(This occurs once you know it is in divine order.)

As I write this, I am coming to believe I was shown this in order to pass it on to as many people as possible that they should commit these four steps to memory immediately in order to have a tool to help them stay strong during the tribulations that appear very likely to occur in the coming months.

When everything around us appears to be breaking down, we will need this 4-Step process to remind us of the divine perfection in the situation and that the breakdown we are experiencing is just a prelude to a breakthrough into a new consciousness and way of being.

Article #2. A World of Forgiveness By 2012

*In the last newsletter and blog entry, I mentioned how all of a sudden, the Emerge-n-See 4-Step Process for Creating Peace in Your Life had come to the fore as the premier tool in the Radical Forgiveness arsenal of tools to be used to transform the energy in any situation. It was a wake-up call for me because, since 2001, I have stated my mission as being: "**To shift the consciousness of the planet through Radical Forgiveness and create a world of forgiveness by 2012.**"*

I realize that 2012 is not necessarily a date certain for dramatic change. Nevertheless, should the necessities of life, to which we have become completely accustomed and take for granted, suddenly, at any time, become very scarce (like a steady supply of food, water, fuel, transportation and other consumer goods), and the structures on which we have always relied to give continuity, predictability and order to life begin to crumble (like the financial system, the legal system and perhaps even government as we know it), we will need spiritual tools that will help us move through the experience with a knowingness that, in spite of how it might look, everything is in divine order.

The Radical Forgiveness worksheet, whether online or on paper, will remain an extremely helpful tool for shifting energy when there is time to reflect and spend the time doing it, and the 13 Steps audio tool will still be perfect to listen to when you are at home or in the car, assuming, that is, you still have fuel to run the car. But the tool that has the most potential for the fulfillment of my mission to create a world of forgiveness, especially during crisis times, is the Emerge-n-See 4-Step Process. That's for the very reasons my students of the Spirituality in Business course gave me. It's memorable and once memorized, it's instantly available exactly when needed – and it works.

If and when such crisis times, as seem to be looming ahead, do actually hit, large numbers of fearful and confused people will probably not be easily persuaded to take the time to learn about and use the Radical Forgiveness worksheet. However, they might, in their anxiety, be willing to reach out and grasp at something as simple as the 4-Step process, if only to see if it worked. I believe it will work for them even if they have never heard of Radical Forgiveness, because it will resonate something deep within them and they will feel a sense of peace when they do it.

My aim, therefore, is to create a mass awareness of the fact that such a simple tool as the Emerge-n-See 4-Step Process can help people get through the difficult times ahead and emerge with a transformed consciousness.

My hope is that you, already having this awareness, will learn the 4 Steps by heart if you haven't already done so and will find ways to teach it to others. If people seem deaf to it now, they won't be when everything around them is breaking down. They will come to you because they will notice that you are not in fear like everyone else and that you always seem to know what to do. (That's because you will be receiving guidance assuming, you are in a peaceful enough state to receive it.)

Article #3. A Question of Vibration

In the previous two postings, I have stressed the need for a tool to help us stay in a place of relative peace even when things are difficult and stressful, and that the tool I recommend is the Emerge-n-See, 4-Step Process for Creating Peace in Your Life. I mentioned in the last posting that if you can stay in a state of relative peace during scary situations you will be in a state to receive guidance about what to do, where to go to be safe and how you can be of assistance to others. That means we must work to keep our vibration high.

169

The book, *Power vs. Force* by David Hawkins, M.D., Ph.D., *provides us with a useful scale by which to gauge our vibratory condition at any one time, relative to the vibratory rate of certain states of being. For example, apathy, guilt and shame are the very lowest, with fear only a few points above them. On the other hand, forgiveness, awareness, understanding and acceptance come high on the scale. Not as high as love, joy and peace, of course, but high enough for someone who can hold such a frequency to counteract many hundreds of thousands who are vibrating at the lowest levels. This is why it is so important that you hold the highest vibration possible.*

The more people there are who understand that the breakdown of all existing structures, forms, belief systems and behaviors that are inconsistent with the principle of Oneness is exactly what is required, the easier it will be. Conversely, the more people there are who descend into panic and refuse to see the perfection in what is happening, the more difficult it will be and the longer it will take for the shift in consciousness to occur.

But will you be able to hold that higher vibration even when things get really bad? Or will you, too, be drawn back down into fear and despondency? This is where tools like the Emerge-n-See 4-Step Process come into play. This, as well as the other Radical Forgiveness tools, all of which calibrate very high, will help you maintain a high vibration even in the worst of circumstances, because they will remind you to hold firm in your vision of the divine perfection in what is occurring. Even in the worst of circumstances, you can expand into the Love vibration.

Maintaining a high vibration will also enable you to receive guidance about where to go, what to do and how best to facilitate the shift. If you are in fear and despondency, you will not be in a state where you can hear the messages given to you by your own

170

spirit guides, guardian angel and others in the angelic realm, who I strongly feel are standing by ready to assist in creating this wonderful vision of heaven on earth. Radical Forgiveness is a form of prayer and a request for help in maintaining a willingness to see the perfection in any situation, and the angels do respond. They will help you, but you will need to be in a state of being where you can hear their whispers.

I feel strongly that whatever is about to happen in the months ahead will become the moment of great awakening, the emergence of humanity into a world of Oneness and the ultimate merging of heaven and earth. We need, therefore, to be able to hold this incredibly joyful vision even as we experience the changes that are necessary to bring it about.

* * * * * * * * *

So learn the 4-Step Emerge-n-See process by heart, and practice it often so it becomes second nature to you. When it has become second nature, you will automatically be defaulting to the Radical Living lifestyle. It could hardly be any easier.

171

15. The Heaven-on-Earth Scenario

Those last two articles raise issues that need some explanation, particularly the reference to the possibility that we are heading towards a severe structural breakdown on a worldwide basis. As you probably know, it had been prophesied at many different times down the centuries and from many different sources that there would be such a breakdown around the year 2012 and that it would be cataclysmic in nature. There also seemed to be broad agreement about how it might look. None of it pleasant. These prophecies appeared in such places as the biblical Book of Revelation as well as the traditional texts of the Mayans, the Hopi Indians and other indigenous peoples.

The best known seer whose predictions have proven to be extremely accurate was Nostradamus. He was born in 1503 and foresaw many global events that have already come true and even now continue to unfold as he predicted. He not only foretold both world wars but actually named Hitler and described the swastika. He foretold the discovery of penicillin, AIDS, the assassination of President Kennedy and the collapse of the Soviet Union. He foretold the people would elect the 'village idiot' as the leader of the most powerful nation in the early part of the third millennium and foresaw cataclysmic change on a global scale at around the same time, including massive earth changes and violent political upheaval. He also spoke of a "King of Terror That Will Come from the Skies." People are still trying to decide whether this refers to the 9/11 event or something worse yet to come.

The Hopi Indians also had many that could see beyond the physical world and see the truth. They too have been extremely accurate in their predictions and have offered humans many a window on the future. They spoke of "Three Great Shakings" that would occur at the end of the millennium and the beginning of the next. Scholars have interpreted this to be the First and Second World Wars.

The thing that is most frequently mentioned with respect to 2012 is the fact that the Mayan calendar comes to an abrupt end on December 21, 2012. Some naively interpreted this to mean the end of the world but, of course, the day came and went without incident. Others have taken it to mean the ending of life as we know it which may be a lot closer to the truth. Who knows?

Edgar Cayce, the much respected healer and clairvoyant, made a number of very precise predictions including the stock market crash of 1929 and the Second World War. Many of his predictions for the new millennium concerned political upheaval on a global scale and 'earth changes' that would be cataclysmic in nature. Many of the predictions say that the upheaval will be a cleansing, analogous to a healing crisis, and that it will be followed by a Great Awakening and a major shift in consciousness. They say that the first phase might involve death and destruction on a massive scale and is likely to last for some years. The second phase they describe as being a sustained period of peace, harmony and tranquility such as humans have never before experienced.

This sounds very much like the process we have been describing for each of our individual soul journeys—a long period of spiritual amnesia that comes to a crescendo with a significant breakdown experience that propels us into an awakening. The only difference is the scale.

The whole human race seems to be creating its own breakdown experience prior to breaking through into the new consciousness. The financial crash of 2008 was the beginning of the breakdown; and at the time of writing, it appears to be ready to happen all over again. Right now, it looks like the calm before the storm.

How this will play out we don't really know. But if it goes according to the prophecies, we shall be moving from a consciousness grounded in fear, separation, greed, guilt and anger, into a realm in which we will be totally aware of our Oneness and will live with one another in peace, love and harmony. We shall be witnessing the death of civilization and the social order as we know it and the birth of a wholly new way of living and being. The long experiment with separation will be over.

If this is true, it seems that the human race has arrived at a point of choice: whether to have the kind of future that involves massive dislocation, pain and death, OR one that offers immediate peace, LOVE and tranquility.

Those of us who are awake will need to be proactive in facilitating this shift into an expansion of Love. We need to engage people in the conversation and give people the awareness of what the choice is, and then provide them with the spiritual technology to render the choices possible to make. This is the purpose of this book.

I believe by using the Radical Transformation tools and taking specific steps to raise your vibration and by settling into an acceptance of the new paradigm in advance of the breakdown, you will be of great assistance in making the shift a relatively

175

smooth one. At no time will it be more important to be able to expand your consciousness in the direction of Love than in such circumstances.

We all need to go into this experience without fear; and the only way to do that is to understand that Love is all there is and that Love will be flowing at all times, no matter what is happening. As long as you stay awake and expanding in Love, you will receive the guidance you will need to stay safe and be of assistance to others.

Those that offer strong resistance might not make it through. A lot of people are going to need help in going through this experience if they are going to keep their vibration high enough to survive. This is why I offer training in Radical Living and The Tipping Method because knowing how to do this using the Radical Living tools is anyone's best hope.

As we saw in Chapter 14, the Radical Living strategy that comes most into play in this regard is *Radical Transformation.* This is where we bring this kind of overall awareness of the perfection in what is happening to world events as they occur. This worksheet is specifically designed to apply the technology of Radical Forgiveness to disturbing events that are happening out there in the world, such as disasters, riots, floods, earthquakes, political and social turmoil, etc. Its purpose is to help you first feel the fear, or whatever other emotions you might be feeling, and then transform those feelings in a way that allows you to expand into Love.

What the Radical Transformation Worksheet asks:

Step #1. Describe what is happening in the world out there that is upsetting to you.

Step #2. Indicate what you are feeling about the situation. (It gives a list, and you check them off as well as suggest others.)

Step #3. In recognizing that we are all likely to have knee-jerk reactions, based in the old paradigm, the worksheet asks you to say what came to mind that was of this quality.

Step #4. Suggest what you might be able to do in some practical way that might make a difference.

Step #5. Read, and speak out loud, the Radical Forgiveness Invocation and the two statements that follow it before signing and dating it.

The Radical Forgiveness Invocation
May we all stand firm in the knowledge and comfort that all things are now, have always been and forever will be in divine order, unfolding according to a divine plan.

And may we truly surrender to this truth whether we understand it or not.

May we also ask for support in consciousness in feeling our connection with the divine part of us, with everyone and with everything, so we can truly say and feel — we are ONE.

Step #6. Speak out loud: Having read the above Radical Forgiveness Invocation, I now realize that what is occurring is perfect, all part of the process of moving from consciousness based on fear and greed to one based on love and harmony, and that by holding the vision of a 'healed' world, I am making a huge contribution to having the shift happen relatively quickly and easily.

Step #7. Speak out loud: I hereby declare that I am willing to hold this higher vibration and to resist all temptation to react to events with fear and despondency. Whenever I feel myself slipping back into fear, I am taking six deep breaths in order to bring myself back to my center and maintain my vibration. I am centered now and have released the need to continue feeling what I was feeling in #2 above. *I choose peace.*

Signed: _____ **Date:** _____

[There is an online interactive version of the Radical Transformation Worksheet available to members of the Radical Living Online Community. To access it, scan the QR Code or go to www.colintipping.com/membership.]

16. Manifesting a New Relationship

Before looking at how best to manifest a new relationship, I would like to first flesh out for you the 4th Radical Living Strategy, Radical Manifestation. This is, after all, the strategy that provides the tool with which to set in motion the process of attracting a mate.

Radical Manifestation uses the Law of Attraction to bring into your experience what you want—in this case, a relationship. Just like Radical Forgiveness, it is a form of secular prayer, and it employs your Spiritual Intelligence to make it work.

While some people dismiss it as mere wishful thinking, quantum physics lends a lot of credence to the idea that we create our own reality with our thoughts and emotions. Looking at what many quantum physicists have said, there is every reason to believe that the power to manifest our reality exists within every one of us.

The way they explain how the Law of Attraction works is to demonstrate that matter can be either a wave or a particle. It, therefore, exists as both pure potential as well as in physical form— real and not real at the same time. The critical factor in bringing it from a state of pure potential (a wave) into physical form (a particle) is consciousness. Our thoughts create reality. What we consciously choose to focus on becomes manifest.

The question remains – what kind of consciousness? Most methods of manifesting rely on re-programming the subconscious mind to do the work. Radical Manifestation, on the other hand, chooses to ignore the stubborn subconscious mind altogether and uses our Spiritual Intelligence instead. This part of our psyche has no resistance to the idea that the Universe is nothing but infinite abundance and that we can use our spiritual power to manifest what we want or need. It can easily access the great sea of abundance and bring forth from there what it is we need.

The Tools
Just as Radical Forgiveness provides tools which activate our Spiritual Intelligence so, too, does Radical Manifestation. They are the key to making it work. Manifesting a partner will serve as a good example of how to go through the process, so let's proceed with it as a way to establish the principles, even if it is not your own priority at this time.

The Six Steps in the Manifestation Process
The first four out of the six steps to Radical Manifestation occur as mental and emotional phenomena. The last two arise out of spiritual practice and are the most difficult to master. They are nevertheless the most important because it is through them that you connect with your Spiritual Intelligence. The steps are:

1. Become aware of the need.

2. Clarify and give precise details of what you want.

3. Visualize actually having it.

4. Feel the emotions of already receiving it.

5. Hand it over completely to Spirit.

6. Drop all attachment to having it.

Step #1: Becoming Aware of What You Want
Strangely enough, this is, for some people, a very difficult step. They seem unable to get clear about what they want. A lot of people also confuse goal-setting with manifestation. Goal setting is about you doing something or achieving something, whereas manifesting is about attracting something to you that you don't already have. And that something needs to be tangible and concrete such that you will be able to recognize it when it shows up. A relationship conforms to those requirements; and for you, if that's what you want to create, item #1 is not a problem.

However, it is a good idea even at this point to ask "Why?" Why do I want this relationship? What need will it satisfy? Is it just to fill a hole in me? Do I feel incomplete without someone to make me feel whole? Do I need someone to take care of me and make me feel safe? Do I need someone to take care of in order to be fulfilled? Am I looking for someone to take care of my kids? Do I need someone because I feel lonely? Do I enjoy life better if I have someone to share it with? Do I need a sexual partner?

These are very important questions to ask yourself before going on to Step 2. How you answer them will determine what specific qualities you want in the person and what you will want out of the relationship. You will need to list them but not judge them. Be totally honest with yourself. At this stage, you want to just notice them and make a note of them. Once you have them all listed, then you can evaluate them and see which of them might indicate that you need to work on yourself a bit more before creating this relationship.

Step #2: Give Precise Details of What You Want
Having become aware of the desire, it is now important that you get very clear about precisely what you are asking for in the way of a relationship. So make a list of all the attributes you want in a mate. Many people have tried this and have been successful in manifesting a good match.

However, you must be careful. I had a friend who did this, and someone showed up who seemed to be the answer to her prayer in every respect. They got married; but soon after, she realized that she had asked for all the right things but forgot to make it a requirement that she should be able to love him! They divorced soon after.

So let it be a true reflection of what you want to see show up in a mate and also what you want the relationship to look like. Be aware, too, of what you bring to the relationship. Make sure it fits your values and honors your values. For what you don't want to show up, make sure you express those things in the positive. In other words, if you don't want someone who is mean with money, ask for generosity and openness around money. It is worth spending a lot of time on making this list and giving it careful consideration.

The Power of the Word and Feelings

Once you know what you want in a mate, and it fits your model of a good relationship, give it word. Whenever you speak something, you give it power. Words have enormous energy behind them, and they are powerfully creative, especially if they are accompanied by emotional energy. So make sure you use words in your statement that evoke feeling.

Once you have made your list and written it all down, read it out loud. This is extremely important. It is even more powerful to read it to someone else, or even better, a group of people so long as they are aligned with you in consciousness. Other people so aligned can magnify the energy quite significantly. If you belong to a PowerShift group (See Appendix II), then tell them what you want. That would be ideal.

Always Present Tense

The subconscious mind has no concept of future. It operates only in the present. Therefore, we must always speak or write everything in the present tense, even if what we say sounds awkward or is grammatically incorrect. Never say, *"I will enjoy having a mate with whom to share my life."* Instead you say, *"I am enjoying having a mate who is joyfully sharing my life now, day by day...."*

Already Done

For similar reasons, you need to speak of your intention as already done and received. If you say, "I want a relationship," you are giving power to the word, "want." You will, therefore, continue to get the result of the word you have empowered – want. Therefore, you must say that you "have" something now. *"It is done."* By saying "It is done," you are aligning with the metaphysical paradigm of reality and with what your Spiritual Intelligence knows to be the truth.

Give it a Time Limit

Having just said that time is not a factor, there is good reason why you would always want to include a time scale in your statement of intention. Though there is no actual lag between something being enfolded in the great sea of infinite possibility and it's coming into material existence, our Spiritual Intelligence probably has no awareness of time either. So it might be oblivious to the idea of "when." If we include it in our statement of intent, it will hear us.

Be careful, though, to ensure that in giving some sort of *"by such and such a time...."* statement, you don't reinforce the idea of future and move the writing out of present tense. That's when the grammar is likely to get weird. For example: *"I have found my perfect life partner by the end of this year."*

Step #3: Visualizing the Desired Relationship

While words are powerful, it is also true that a picture is worth a thousand words. Forming a picture in your mind of what your relationship will look like is another way of getting clarity and will give the intention more power. More importantly, however,

183

building a picture in your mind is another way of saying that it is done, especially if it helps you activate the emotions you would feel when the real thing shows up.

So make sure when you build your picture that you include in it elements that give it a "now" meaning, not a future meaning. The picture should say "It is here now." You can also increase the power of the picture by enlarging it to an enormous size. Give it sound as well, and make those sounds good and loud. Make it a rousing performance with as much kinesthetic, visual and aural stimulation as possible.

Step #4: Feel the Emotions of Already Being In the New Relationship

Emotion is a key element in the manifestation process – not just feelings like the excitement of anticipation and expectation but the feelings that arise when you realize your partner is now in your life. What would you be feeling in that moment? Just imagine it and see if you can generate these feelings. Then attach the feelings to the words that you used to articulate what you wanted in the relationship (Step 2). The effect of this is to strongly reinforce the idea that what you have asked for has been given already.

Step #5: Hand it Over Completely to Spirit

What we will have done with the first four steps might be helpful to anyone working from either the old paradigm or the new one; but from here on, the process definitely depends on a willingness to work under the assumptions of the metaphysical paradigm to the exclusion of those belonging to the current 'scarcity' paradigm. This is also the part where *Radical Manifestation* becomes a matter of spiritual practice rather than mental gymnastics.

It is where we say "Thank you" to our conscious mind for supporting us thus far by giving us the words, the pictures and the emotions; but from this point on, we refuse to accept from it any further involvement. Whatever chatter the mind puts forth from now on, we pay no attention whatsoever. We are now working with, and deferring to, a higher authority; and we access it, not through our mind, but through our Spiritual Intelligence. Having put quite a bit of energy into determining our intentions, clarifying them, articulating them and feeling the emotions, the task now is to give it over entirely to one's Higher Self. Only it knows what is best for us.

However, we must be careful here. This is not a recipe for apathy, inaction or a fatalistic attitude. We don't just do nothing and leave it to Spirit to take care of everything. The principle here is co-creation, not dependence. So, for you, this means doing what you have to do to create opportunities to meet people, dating online maybe or going out to places and being active in your life. This is where the goal setting might come in. For example, you might set a goal to make it a point to spend 2 hours a week online, meeting people. Goals are things you are in control of, whereas in the case of manifestation, it is Spirit, through your Higher Self, that decides. And it must be in your divine plan for it to work. That brings me to the last step.

Step #6: Dropping All Attachment to Having the Relationship. This is the hardest step of all. Having spent a lot of energy generating the desire, visualizing and feeling the joy of finally having someone wonderful in your life, you then have to give up your need to have it? Bummer! That's really hard. But this is crucial because in dropping your attachment to having the relationship be a certain way, you get yourself out of the way. This puts you into a state of 'allowing' it to happen instead of 'making' it happen.

However, we might as well admit it; this step is virtually beyond our capacity as a human being to achieve. Step Five is hard enough, but this is almost impossible. But remember, you only have to be *willing* to drop your attachment to having it. So, let that be the practice. Keep telling yourself that you are willing to have no attachment to having it. But don't confuse non-attachment with resignation or being disconnected. Letting go is not 'giving up.'

OK. So that's the process. But I would like to suggest some 'rules' you might wish to follow in order to ensure that the relationship you manifest will bring about the kind of expansion into Love that you want.

Rule #1. *Leave a significant amount of time between leaving one relationship and even thinking about creating another.*

It takes a lot more time than you think to energetically disengage from the previous relationship, especially if it was deep and long-standing and even more especially if the separation was painful. If there were children involved, the problem becomes even more compounded. If you leap straight into another relationship, the chances are very high that you will take into the new relationship all the unresolved issues you had in the old one, recreating the very same set of dynamics that might have been the cause of the breakup in the last relationship.

I realize, of course, that in many cases, meeting another person and falling in love with him or her may have precipitated the breakup. In that case, there might already be a new relationship in existence even before the old one is finished. Nevertheless, a wise couple will still arrange things so that each has a chance to live alone for a good while before moving in with each other. I would suggest at least 6 months and, better yet, one year for the reasons I give in Rule #4 below.

As I mentioned previously, men seem to have the greatest need to find a new partner as quickly as possible and often will force an earlier hook-up than wisdom would normally dictate. He will be even more urgent if he is looking for a mother for his children, assuming he has any. So it will probably be the woman who has to resist the urge to move in together and to insist on having the amount of time she needs to be alone. If he is not willing to allow that, then that should be a red flag anyway. He's not worth having.

Rule #2. *Do the forgiveness work on your previous partner before you begin manifesting a new one.*

And I don't mean just doing one worksheet. You keep doing them until there is no energy left in the situation: no anger, no resentment, no jealousy, no pain, no regrets. This takes some work, obviously, but if you want your new relationship to work, it is essential that you release all those energies. This is why you need to have a lot of time on your own to do this work and to know who you are before you create the new one. There are many people who have never lived on their own for any length of time and, therefore, have no idea who they are separate from another. How can you expand into Love if you don't know who you are and feel less than whole without a partner?

Even if it has been a number of years since your last relationship ended and you have wanted to manifest a new one for a while now, you may still need to do the forgiveness work on your previous partner. The fact that you may still have some energy left there may be the very reason why you haven't been able to attract the new partner.

Rule #3. *Be clear about what you want and don't want in a relationship.*

Use the questionnaire and worksheet in Chapter 6 to establish your values and your boundaries. Get very clear on them and resolve never to compromise on them.

187

When you come to do the Radical Manifestation worksheet, you will be asked to list the attributes you want to have in the person you will be manifesting, so the more thought you put in to this, the better. Think long and hard about what you feel are the most important things you will want in your relationship?

Rule #4. *Scope your partner out over a period of at least 6 - 12 months before committing. Be a detective.*

I described earlier how, in order to create a relationship that would produce a lot of karmic units for both parties, you attract into your life someone who seems absolutely perfect. Then once you have reached a certain stage of intimacy (into-me-see) and you have become hooked, the person begins to reveal the real man or woman behind the mask. Suddenly the person becomes quite opposite to what you thought, and the relationship looks like being a disaster.

I can't tell you how many times I have heard the story of someone finding their 'soul-mate' – the perfect partner who is loving and caring – and then after six months, they turn into a tyrant. It's a great way to produce the experience of separation, of course, but this is not what you want to manifest this time.

So, if you begin dating someone, stay alive to this possibility and do not commit to a full-fledged relationship until you have reached this stage in the relationship where you each have become comfortable enough with each other that you begin to be real. Then watch out for any changes in his or her behavior. They may be subtle at first, but there might be an outburst or two that will give you a hint of what may come later.

You might recall that there are three possible ways in which you might respond to this switch. The first is to recognize that if the new behavior crosses your boundaries and goes against your values, you leave the relationship immediately.

The second is you commit to a further trial period to see if the behavior, now having been brought to the light, will disappear once you have clearly stated your boundaries and made it clear what you want and don't want. The big trap here, though, is to imagine that you have the power to change the person. You do not.

It is very common that women say to themselves, "If I love him enough, he will change and will become what I want him to be." It never happens, so please abandon that strategy right away.

This option, then, is only viable if you are willing to watch to see if the behavior disappears completely within a 12 month period. If it does not, this means the relationship is potentially troubled, and you should consider letting it go.

The third option is to settle. This is where, because your need for a relationship is so strong, you are willing to put up with it so long as he/she stays with you. This option should only be taken if you wish to experience a lot more pain and suffering.

One of my clients who had experienced this 'personality switch,' a couple of times and felt determined not to have it happen again, called the man's ex-wife and asked her what he was like deep down. His ex-wife was only too happy to tell her everything - both good and bad. She learned a lot from her, and they actually became quite good friends as a result. My client eventually married the guy, and it turned out fine. This is a risky strategy, but it is one way of finding out whether there is a hidden side to this person. You really don't know anyone until you live with them, so it's worth asking someone who has done so before you risk it yourself.

Creating a New Relationship Worksheet

1. I have a high intention to manifest someone (a man/woman) with whom to have a loving relationship by _____ (set a time frame).

2. The reasons I am creating this relationship now are:

_____

_____

_____

3. Check the values from the list below that you feel are important values for your partner to have. Then circle the five most important "must have" ones.

☐ loyalty ☐ honesty ☐ fidelity ☐ trust ☐ humility ☐ desire for children ☐ sense of humor ☐ tolerance ☐ my spirituality ☐ sensitivity ☐ self-reliance ☐ strength ☐ willingness ☐ integrity ☐ drive ☐ competitive ☐ caring

Other _____ Other _____

Expand on the five 'must-have' values, saying why they are important and what they mean to you.

a) _____

_____

_____

b) _____

_____

_____

c)

_____

_____

_____

d)

_____

_____

_____

e)

_____

_____

_____

4. What other qualities and attributes you would like to see in your ideal partner and as features of your relationship:

_____

_____

5. Check which of the following values or qualities YOU bring to the relationship? Then, circle the ones you would definitely not compromise over, no matter what.

☐ loyalty ☐ honesty ☐ fidelity ☐ trust ☐ humility ☐ desire for children ☐ sense of humor ☐ tolerance ☐ my spirituality ☐ sensitivity ☐ self-reliance ☐ strength ☐ willingness ☐ integrity ☐ drive ☐ competitive ☐ caring

6. List the other qualities, attributes and resources that YOU can and would bring to a relationship.

_____

_____

7. Now close your eyes and imagine yourself in relationship with the person of your dreams and use all your 'imaginal' senses in a much expanded and exaggerated way to have the full sensation of having the relationship NOW. *In your imagination:*

What you see is: _____

_____

What you hear is: _____

_____

What you smell is:_____

_____

What you taste is: _____

_____

What you feel (touch) is:_____

_____

Give voice to these sensations and build a 'huge' picture in your mind and begin to feel yourself expanding in Love as a result of having the relationship as your reality now.

[To see me demonstrating this on a video and suggesting a somewhat outrageous method of leveraging this even more, scan here or go to www.ExpandinginLove.com]

7. Say these statements out loud and with conviction:

a) I now realize and acknowledge that my Spiritual Intelligence and the Universe may have something in mind for me other than what I have asked for. I, therefore, give it over to Spirit and surrender totally to what may come.

b) I now, therefore, declare my total trust of the Universe to give me what is for my highest good, and I feel love and gratitude for the Spirit that is within me and all things.

c) I completely surrender to Spirit now and drop all attachment to having a relationship show up in any particular way, knowing that it is done and I shall recognize the perfection of it when I see it.

d) I feel myself totally reconnected with my Source and know that I am in the midst of pure abundance. I am open to receive that abundance continually.

"It Is Done - And So It Is!"

Note: There is a fully interactive version of this worksheet on the Radical Living Online Community website. (See Appendix III)

193

17: Radical Money

I cannot leave this section on Radical Living without saying something about money, even at the risk of being accused of repeating some of what I have already written in my other book, *Radical Manifestation: The Fine Art of Creating the Life You Want*, and in the Manual of the Online Radical Money Program. Even if we do all the forgiveness work and the self-forgiveness work we need to do and find some measure of success in manifesting things, and yet fail to adjust our consciousness around money, we will not be able to achieve a high level of vibration consistent with the Radical Living lifestyle.

Neither will we truly expand in Love if we remain in fear around money, which is how most of us relate to it now, living as we do in the prevailing fear-based paradigm. We give our power over to money and we let it define who we are. We use money to symbolize power, status, social standing and success, all of which are subject to being taken away in an instant because they are not real. People say they love money, but they really hate it because they are so afraid of losing it.

During the spiritual amnesia phase, money clearly serves us well in enabling us to create all manner of separation pain. However, if we are to achieve any level of spiritual awareness within the context of the Radical Living philosophy, we need to move away from all these fear-based attitudes around money and adopt those that are more in line with the new paradigm. The following assumptions are listed in the Radical Manifestation book, but it's worth it to repeat them here since they are fundamental to a raised consciousness around money. They are as follows:

Money has no inherent value. It only has value when it is exchanged for something of real value, and then it ceases to be money anyway. Getting money is not an end in itself. What is important is the purpose to which you put it.

Money is energy. Money is as much subject to the Law of Attraction as any other sort of energy. It will flow naturally towards those who are the most willing to receive it, have a use for it, and have no problem asking for it in exchange for something of value.

There is no shortage of money. Since money is energy and energy is limitless, money is also limitless. Right now, there's a ton of it in circulation — more than you can ever imagine. And they keep printing more of it. The more people there are on the planet, the more money there is. It keeps multiplying. There is as much money in the system as the system demands. The more we give it, lend it, spend it and create value with it, the more it expands.

Abundance is the natural condition of the Universe. The idea of infinite abundance is fundamental to a Radical Living money consciousness. Most of what we like to have is free anyway. Money is not needed for such things as sunshine, rain, a smile, a cheerful word, a touch, a kiss, a birdsong, the smell of a flower and so on. Actually, when you begin to think about it, only a very small amount of what we really love about life comes about through having money. Once you have your food and a warm, comfortable place to live in, the rest is relative.

Money has no power. When we become aware of the power that we have to create the circumstances of our lives, we realize that we are no more at the mercy of money than we are of any outer circumstance. The real source of our power lies within, and there is not a single person on this planet who is denied access to that. We are all equally powerful in that regard, no matter how much money we have.

Money gives us freedom to choose. It is true that the more money we have, the more choices we can make about how we live. However, it is the choices that one makes which determine happiness, not the amount of money one has.

Money is our teacher. As spiritual beings having a human experience, we are blessed with the ability to experience life and access our power through our feelings. Money provides many opportunities to feel our feelings and, through such experiences, to grow and learn. It is not a matter of whether or not you have money; it's how you feel about it that is important.

Your Money Consciousness History

We now know that consciousness creates reality. This being so, if you want to know what your consciousness is around a particular thing, look at how it shows up in your life. Look back at your money history to see how this has worked in your life up to now and then decide how you wish to relate to money from now on.

Just as you have done in previous chapters, construct a timeline; but this time, plot your income over the years until now. Take the time to be as accurate as you can with this — especially in plotting the highs and the lows. Not only will it show you what your money blueprint looks like, but it will also provide you with your subconscious 'income set point,' beyond which your subconscious mind will not let you go but once, if at all. This will also count as your starting point for the ***Online X4 Money Program,*** should you decide to do it. That program is designed to raise your set point over a period of a year so that by the end of two years your income should have increased four times.

> *[The Online X4 Money Program is designed to quadruple your income within 2 years. Scan the QR code or go to www.colintipping.com/online-programs.]*

Whatever the pattern is, it serves as an indication of your money consciousness. And you need to understand that you alone are the creator and controller of it. Notice where your 'comfort level' is and whether, as in the following example, you had a 'spike' that went beyond the comfort zone but was never repeated.

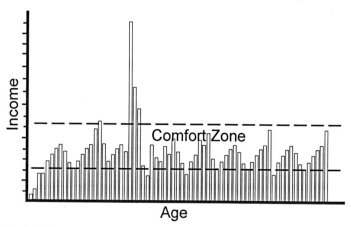

Fig. 7: Your Money History

Assuming your pattern looks something like this, the question then becomes, what part of your consciousness made you stay within that comfort zone and limited the flow of money beyond it? What part of you decided never to repeat the one big spike because it felt painful to go so far beyond your set point?

The answer is, of course, your subconscious mind. Deep down, you have whole series of beliefs and assumptions about money that you learned at an early age from your parents and from your social environment. These beliefs are like little gyroscopes always working to keep you in line with your comfort zone as defined in your money blueprint. Which of the following do you recognize as being part of your money consciousness?

☐ You have to work hard for money.

☐ Money does not grow on trees.

☐ I have to struggle for money.

☐ Money is a scarce commodity.

☐ Money is the root of all evil.

☐ Behind every fortune, there is a great crime.

☐ I can't ask for money.

☐ Money brings too many problems.

☐ Money is for the upper classes.

☐ People with money are suspect   .

Other_____

Money & Social Class
One factor that helps determine your money consciousness is the social class and culture into which you were born. This will have a great bearing on your money consciousness, even if you have become socially mobile (hopefully upwards) since then.

199

The link between money and class varies from country to country. In America, for example, the link between money and success, status and power is relatively strong. It is an essential part of the American dream that anyone, no matter where they come from, can become prosperous through hard work and perseverance. Therefore, anyone who "makes it" in America is well thought of and can easily rise up to the next class. What class you are in does not limit your income potential so much as in other countries though it is clearly an advantage to come from a rich family.

That is not so true for England. Where you went to school, how you speak, your family connections, what your father did for a living, etc., means a lot more than how much money you have. Worse yet, they are factors that follow you throughout your life, irrespective of future income. Paradoxically, however, what social class you are in has a very strong influence over one's expectations of how much money you are likely to earn. It is very subtle and complicated; but the class system has a great effect on people's money consciousness, and it is much more difficult to overcome than in America.

Even in America, the terms 'Working Class,' 'Blue Collar,' and even 'Middle Class' connote certain ideas of the likely income levels of each. The vast majority of those in these categories, especially the first two, are likely to be people with "jobs" as opposed to being in business for themselves. And we all know that very few people get rich working a job all their life. (Some CEOs excepted.)

Each social class has a 'collective money consciousness,' which means that there is an agreed set of beliefs, attitudes, expectations and limitations that everyone in that class holds and subscribes to about work and money, albeit unconsciously. Anyone who steps outside of that collective ideal will experience reactions from others to a greater or lesser degree.

So, just try to be aware of the degree to which your social class has had an effect on your money consciousness. If it has been very positive and supportive of your having wealth and high levels of income, be grateful. If it has had a tendency to keep you limited, you need to decide what it is you have to do to counteract it, hopefully without losing friends and creating tension within your family by appearing to be 'moving away from your roots,' or becoming 'superior,' or 'better than.' Moving up the social ladder can definitely press some 'loyalty buttons' with friends and family.

Money and Values

The meaning that money and wealth will have for you and the ways in which it will add value to your life are, to a large extent, governed by the meaning you give your own life. This is likely to change according to current circumstances and what stage of life you are at. What is important to you and a priority in your twenties is almost certainly going to be different to when you are in your sixties.

Now, to some degree, it may be that life has been defined for you by the limitations imposed by your financial circumstances. If you were dirt-poor, living in an impoverished community, then life's meaning is likely to have been little more than mere survival. On the other hand, if you were brought up in a very wealthy family, the source of income being a family business handed down from generation to generation, it might be that your life's meaning was defined for you around being the next leader of the family firm, whether it was a fit for you or not. It is unlikely that you would be living your true purpose in either circumstance because you didn't choose it.

201

Yet there might have been a measure of comfort in either situation since, because your life was, in a sense, defined for you, you didn't have to think beyond that. However, when you embrace the Radical Living lifestyle, you will need to start taking responsibility for making your own life. And for that, you need a sense of purpose.

This is important because without a strong sense of purpose, money will have very little real value to you. Money for its own sake is valueless. It's what you do with money that matters and what you do with it depends on your values. And what your values are tend to define who you are and sets the purpose for your life, especially once you have awakened. Prior to then, you were more likely to have focused more on making money for fear-based reasons. But now, your values may have changed. As we have seen, it is likely that being of service is more appealing and potentially fulfilling and that the purpose of having money is to support that dream. Bill Gates, the CEO of Microsoft and one of the most richest people on the planet, is a good example of this. He is using the billions of dollars he has to bring healing to millions of people on the planet.

So, what is your purpose? Do you have a dream to fulfill? A mission, perhaps? Or not? Are you currently fulfilled in your work or life? What's missing? Did you give up a dream to accommodate someone else's needs or demands? Did you trade a dream for safety, conformity, love, money, status, power? Are you searching for a purpose? Is this the time to go for it?

[In my book, *Getting to Heaven on a Harley*, I outline the process of living your purpose. I won't repeat it here, but it does provide a way to discover your purpose, create a vision, set goals and objectives and move into right action using spiritual principles.]

However, whatever purpose you discover for yourself will be secondary to just being who you are. That is your primary purpose. Everything else is secondary. So, focus on expanding into Love and on just being Love, no matter what you are doing as your 'purpose.'

There's a true story about a particular ward in a hospital in which no matter who went there as patients and no matter what their illnesses were, they all improved quite dramatically. For weeks, the authorities tried to determine what the difference was and could find no answer. Finally, they discovered that what made the difference was that the person who cleaned the floors on that ward was someone who exuded loving energy. She said little or nothing as she worked. She just was Love. That was her purpose and she was living it, quietly and with humility.

That said, however, our human journey may well involve other specific intentions of a spiritual nature that we have agreed to take on, either before incarnating or to be gathered during our lifetime. These are definitely secondary to the primary one of just being human, but they can give our lives added meaning in human terms. They are usually oriented towards serving others in some profound and meaningful way and can involve the sharing of one's particular gifts and talents.

A Buddhist monk known to a very good friend of mine, Darryl Dennis, said something that changed her life and gave Darryl her life's mission. He said, *"Every person must be given the opportunity to contribute a part of him/herself to something bigger than him/herself at least once during his or her lifetime. If not they will feel that their life has been without meaning or purpose."* Ever since that moment, Darryl's mission has been to teach people to contribute to others and to show that simply having the intention to give value is a powerful business strategy.

Once you have completed your analysis and determined the nature of your money blueprint, then you can begin the process of creating a new one. However, it is not a matter of trying to change the existing blueprint in the subconscious mind. It can only be done if you use your Spiritual Intelligence to override it completely. You do this by adopting the spiritually based assumptions listed at the beginning of this chapter. For this, you use the Money Consciousness Worksheet in conjunction with the Radical Manifestation worksheet. It is only by using these tools, and the 13 Steps audio processes that augment the worksheets, that the shift can be achieved. (See Appendix 1 for the list of tools.)

In time, you will develop an unshakeable trust that, since there is no shortage of money, your needs will always be met and that you will be abundantly supplied at all times. Instead of being fearful about money, you will begin relating to money with happiness and joy, no matter how much is flowing in your life at any one time.

This is because you realize that you have a natural ability to attract money whenever you need it, enabling you to live your purpose, manifest your dreams and embrace the Radical Living approach to life and money. You will become very open to receiving money from whatever source and have a high need to share it abundantly with others, or use it in ways that make a difference to others as well as yourself. You will experience the joy of being generous with money, knowing that there's plenty more in the spiritual pipeline. Finally, you will find yourself having no attachment to money because you know it will always manifest when needed.

But shifting your consciousness around money to this degree takes practice and constant awareness of your feelings and thoughts whenever you are dealing with money, especially when you are at risk of going beyond your income set point, or operating outside of your comfort zone. At this time, there are very few people who can truly operate from this paradigm of total abundance, so you will need to be patient with yourself.

Practice creating money frequently using the worksheets, but begin by asking for modest amounts at first that would be within your comfort zone to receive; and always say what you want the money for and by when. It is also a rule that if the money shows up, you must use it for the purpose intended. Do not divert it to some other purpose no matter how important it seems to be; otherwise you will block all further supply. Just do a separate Radical Manifestation worksheet on that one.

Practice enlightened spending. By that, I mean use money wisely, of course, and stay out of debt at all costs. But beyond that, be generous with it. Leave big tips. Always buy the best wherever possible and use money in a way that brings you joy. Travel first class whenever you have the chance. Buy expensive presents for those you love. Give money away. Use money in ways that lift your spirit and feed your soul, like going to concerts, creating a beautiful environment at home, paying other people to do the things you are not good at or hate to do, and so on. Spend consciously and with gay abandon. Why not? There's no shortage of money. (Note: That's not the same as using a credit card to cover money you don't have. We, and every country in the world, should have learned that lesson by now.)

A lot of people scrimp and scrape and then hoard money solely in order to pass it all on to their children when they die. I feel very ambivalent about that idea. I've always said, in jest of course, that I want to die at 95, totally broke, having just spent my very last penny on consuming a Havana cigar and a large brandy and having just been accused of making (successful) sexual overtures to a beautiful woman. In other words, having lived my life fully, without restriction and leaving nothing behind.

Of course, if you do have a lot of money left over after having used money in an enlightened, Radical Living sort of way and have not shortchanged yourself (or others near and dear to you) in any way up to the point of your passing, then it's fine to leave the residue to your kids. But to imagine that to be the main purpose of your having money is old paradigm thinking. If you want to see your children more abundant, give them money as and when you feel like it. That way, you get to feel the joy of giving, and they see you modeling how to keep money moving in your life and hopefully will learn from your example.

Remember, money sitting in the bank has little or no value. It is just a few numbers in columns on a computer. If your kids are still operating in the old paradigm, the chances are that what you leave them might be more than their income set point allows, in which case they will find a way to get rid of it very quickly. That happens all the time. Worse yet, the siblings might fight over it and become mortal enemies. That is also very common.

Obviously, the subject of money is a big one and, from a Radical Living point of view, a massively important one for us to get; and I have only touched the surface in this chapter. If and when we do find ourselves in a period where the financial system breaks down completely and we have chaotic conditions prevailing where the money becomes virtually useless, our trust in the Universe to meet our needs and keep us abundantly supplied will become our most valuable survival mechanism. All of a sudden, we will finally get it that money is meaningless and, in such circumstances, pretty much irrelevant.

PART FOUR

CLEARING OUT AND CLEANING UP

18. Deconstructing Your Stories

Shifting from one paradigm to the next is like moving house. Whether you like it or not, you're forced to go through every room in the house and pull it apart, empty every cupboard and closet, and make decisions about what to keep and what to throw away.

As you begin the process, you begin to realize just how much stuff you have stored away over the years at the back of closets, under beds, in the garage, in the basement and in the loft. You may feel extremely loathe to relieve yourself of those things to which you may have strong attachments, even though you know you will never use them again. Family heirlooms present particular problems. Will they fit the new house? Can I bear to part with them knowing how much they meant to my forebears? Would I be letting them, and my family, down if I sold them? What about all those old photos of departed ones that remind us of the past, both good and bad?

While it is true that when you move house, you absolutely have to clear everything out of the house and give it a good clean before you leave, people who shift paradigms have a tendency to forget that they also need to do the same. They sneak away leaving behind a lot of their old victim stories, painful memories and habits of being, tucked away in closets out of sight and out of their (conscious) mind. A few things might have been taken out and given a quick polish, but nevertheless returned to the cupboard and then forgotten.

But are they dead? No, they fester still, and when the time is right, the old stories will ooze out of their box and re-infect lives in ways hardly imagined.

As I have said before, I am assuming you are now either in the awakening phase or well beyond it. I am also assuming that you are relatively comfortable with the idea that we come here to experience the opposite of Oneness as a part of our spiritual evolution, and also, that the separation experiment is close to being over and the end-game is 'heaven-on-earth.' But even this is no guarantee that you haven't still got stashed away in your own basement, a lot of old stuff that still has its origins in the previous paradigm. Memories of being hurt, abused, betrayed and abandoned; losses that you've never properly grieved; the abortion you still feel guilty about; and the pain you inflicted on your kids or partner, and so on.

You may have some items nicely polished with *'spiritual bypass lotion'* and wrapped in flimsy *old-style forgiveness wrapping;* but like all the other stuff in that stinky old closet, it still owns you. It still has the power to pull you back into that old paradigm and keep you stuck in Victimland. I can't tell you how many times people say to me, "Oh, I've done my work on that issue," or "Yes, I've forgiven my father," and then—when their buttons are pushed—regress right back into the same old story and relive the pain.

Of course, anyone might be forgiven for imagining that, having awakened, they are home free and able to go on their merry way full of joy and love, without ever looking back. A lot of spiritual programs promote this idea, implying that all you need to do is meditate your way out of it and use a bunch of airy-fairy affirmations to make you feel good. Meanwhile, your stuff in the closet continues to fester and grow, ready to break free and wreak havoc, even if you have awakened, and no less so if you have been awake for a long time.

The fact is that there remains some important clean-up work to do before we can truly say we are ready to live consciously and expand into Love. Unless that old stuff, that served us so well during the spiritual amnesia phase of our life, is truly neutralized and transformed, it will continue to come back and bite us.

Again, it's all about energy. If you still have it invested in the stories of what happened, or you still have repressed emotional holdings about things that occurred which were painful, or beliefs about how you were victimized in some way, expectations that were not realized, promises that weren't kept, judgments you are still holding, and so on, that energy will continue to magnetize you back to that time and keep you tagged into that karma.

All these energies associated with the first phase of your life have to be cleaned out and dispersed (albeit with love and gratitude) before you can really begin expand into Love in a meaningful way, and without the risk of being pulled back. If you are going to really move forward and begin to manifest the life you want for yourself and contribute to the overall raising of mass consciousness, you need to have your energy, not in the past, but fully in present time.

Exercise
Imagine you have just awakened, emerged from what you now realize was Victimland, and are ready to move into your new way of being. Being honest and truthful with yourself now, you admit that you have a whole lot of stories, mostly of the

victim or perpetrator variety, stored away in the attic, and they need clearing out. So, you enter that dark, rather smelly attic and therein notice the boxes in which all those victim/perpetrator stories have been carefully stored away and hidden well out of view. Open each box and see what's inside. Then carefully make a list of the stories contained in them.

1. _____

2. _____

3. _____

4. _____

5. _____

6. _____

7. _____

8. _____

9. _____

10. _____

As you sort through them, you are realizing that you are still rather attached to quite a few of them. As you list them, you are not altogether sure which of them are still active in your life even now and which are not. There are also some you had even forgotten about or had repressed at the time each story was born. You notice, too, that some still weigh heavily upon you, depending on how long ago they happened and how much 'work' has been done already (you think) to reduce the energy attached to them.

People often tell me they've done a lot of work on their stories and have completed the forgiveness work on them, too. But if they have only used conventional forgiveness, then the chances are that much of the original pain is still there, albeit deeply buried.

I say that because with conventional forgiveness, there is no requirement that you give up the idea that you have been victimized. Even though you try to forgive, you still believe that something wrong happened. Therefore, the desire to forgive is counter-balanced by a need to condemn the person for having done something to you. Unfortunately, when push comes to shove, the need to condemn wins hands down every time. The forgiveness, therefore, remains a very thin and delicate veneer, especially if we are talking about something very serious.

Notice which stories are connected and have been leveraged into a repetitive pattern as previously described on Page 34. Even if they are not part of a pattern, all victim/perpetrator stories have much the same distinctive structure. At the center is the actual event: What happened. Around that is the emotional pain associated with it. That usually accounts for about 10% of the story because we would have leveraged that pain into suffering by 'awfulizing' and adding a whole bunch of erroneous assumptions, beliefs and interpretations around the story. We leveraged it still further by looking for people to blame and vowed we could not be happy until we had revenge. (We call it justice, but it's revenge we really want.) That's the other 90%.

[It may be worth taking a moment to review the video that was initially referenced on Page 34 regarding this dynamic. It is an important piece. Go to www.ExpandinginLove.com or scan the code to watch it again.]

The first step, then, in dissolving the energy that holds a story together is to identify those assumptions and beliefs used in its construction in order to get back to that 10% core. Then in the following chapters we shall explore how to neutralize them.

Stripping them all out of the story will at least collapse it down to a more truthful version of what actually happened and will make the process of reframing the story, which is the next big step, a lot easier.

19. Repudiating the Beliefs

Most of our belief systems have been handed down from generation to generation. Linked together, they constitute not only our world view but the very ideas about how reality is constructed. As we have seen, these have a strong bias at all levels towards a world view which supports the idea that we are victims of our circumstances and more or less powerless over our lives.

This might have been very helpful in enabling us to create separation, but such beliefs remain very difficult to break even if we have awakened and begun to shift into the new paradigm. Given the state of our consciousness, we are still very insecure in this paradigm and have yet to anchor it deep into our way of being. Our hold on this new vision of reality is tenuous at best, so it's not surprising that we are reluctant to let go of our long-held beliefs.

However, the best we can do, at this particular moment, is to cast our minds back to the time before we were awake and do our best to identify, and then repudiate, the beliefs we once held to be true but which now have no validity. In the beginning, we used our rational conscious minds to do this, all the while knowing that the subconscious mind might well resist our efforts and seek to reinforce the old beliefs. That's OK, though, because the real transformation will come when we use our Spiritual Intelligence to reframe the stories and automatically dump the beliefs that held them together. That's when the whole structure will crumble and dissolve once and for all. But first, we need to discover what those beliefs are.

The problem with trying to identify core-negative beliefs is that they tend to be unconscious. You hardly know that they are there, much less what they actually say. However, one way to identify them is to work backwards. What you do is look back at what keeps showing up in your life and then deduce from that what the belief must be that's creating that kind of activity. Look at your list of stories and see what's there. The principle here is whatever turns up 'out there,' especially if it is repeated over and over again, is an outplaying of what is 'in here.'

If all sorts of people consistently treat you a certain way, then you can safely assume that they are energetically picking up on some belief you have about yourself and that they are subconsciously treating you in alignment with that belief. For example, if people tend to ignore you all the time, then you probably have a belief that you are not worth listening to, or that you have nothing worthwhile to say, or that you are a boring person. If people continually let you down, you probably have a belief that says, "People always betray me," or "People don't value me."

If you have read my book, *Radical Forgiveness*, you will recall from Chapter One that my sister, Jill, based her whole life on the belief that she would never be enough for any man. That belief came from her original wound of feeling unloved by her father.

Exercise:
Go back over your list of stories and try to identify what we call the 'core-negative' beliefs that lay behind each of your stories. Review the patterns that were revealed plus any others

that have come to mind since, and see if you can deduce a few probable beliefs that you might have been acting out over the years. Then write down variations on what you think those core-negative beliefs might be. To get you started, here a few examples of typical core-negative beliefs:

I will never be enough.

It is not safe to be me.

I am always last or left out.

People always abandon me.

It is not safe to speak out.

I should have been a boy.

I'll never make it.

Life is not fair.

No matter how hard I try, it is never enough.

I am unworthy.

I'll never be successful.

It is not good to be powerful/successful/rich/outgoing.

I don't deserve . . .

I must always obey or suffer.

I am alone.

Other people are more important than me.

No one will love me.

I am unlovable

No one is there for me.

I have to do it all myself.

Other:

Complete your list of "likely" beliefs. Then look through them and pick out the ones that seem to you to have the most resonance. Write them up here or in a journal and then write each one on a separate Post-it or piece of paper. Put them to one side.

You might find this next step counterintuitive and perhaps difficult to imagine, but I want you to feel love and acceptance for each one of the beliefs. Yes, I did say "**love**" them! Love them as part of who you have been up to now, and then remain open to the possibility that they have served you in some way. Love them for what they have done for you, even if you can't see it.

It's important to love them because beliefs are not just benign things that exist as connections in the brain which can be turned off just like that. They exist as an integral part of your Self. That means, if you make the beliefs wrong and try to get rid of them, you are actually attacking and undermining your own Self. That's a big deal. Bringing Love to the situation by loving yourself for having the belief, and loving the belief itself prior to disavowing it, will quiet your 'Inner Judge' and make your mind more receptive to the idea that there was a purpose in having it at some time in your life, but no longer. So you can let it go.

I'm sure you've heard of the saying, "What you resist, persists." Right? It's certainly applicable in this instance. If you resist the energy by trying to release it from a place of judgment, it will become stronger.

If you love it just the way it is, accepting it as having been a loving supportive part of yourself you now see as no longer relevant to your life, it will dissolve on its own. It will cease to have any vote in your reality; and from this point on, it will have no power to create circumstances in your life that would normally have supported the belief.

So, I hope you can now see that to ask "How do I get rid of these beliefs?" is to ask the wrong question. The real question is, "How can I get to a point where I can lovingly accept my belief, and love myself completely for having it, so I can let it dissolve naturally?"

Action. Take those pieces of paper on which you wrote your beliefs and, one by one, do the following.

1. Hold the belief in your left hand (which connects it to your right brain), hold it high, and then say this, with feeling:

   "I love myself for having had the belief that . . . . and realize that this belief has served me lovingly in the past. I send love and appreciation now to this belief and the part of my ego that has felt the need to hold onto it. I feel blessed to have had it as part of my consciousness until this moment and realize now that I need to hold onto it no longer. **I, therefore, lovingly release it from my consciousness NOW."**

2. Now hold the belief in your right hand and say the same thing again, this time connecting with your left brain.

[To watch a video of me doing this same process as part of the 'Satori' Radical Forgiveness Game, scan the QR code here or go to www.ExpandinginLove.com.]

Repeat steps 1 and 2 three times, changing hands each time; and say the last line with gusto and plenty of voice. Put some physical energy behind it as well. Then, when you have finished doing it for that one belief, tear the paper up or burn it.

20. Expectations & Judgments

It often comes as a great shock to people to discover that much of the pain that drives their story comes from believing that someone did not meet their expectations. They are upset and displeased that the person did not behave in the way they expected and did not meet their demands. They also wanted the person to be different to the way they were.

The main feeling directly associated with an unmet expectation is disappointment. But it can also include anger and frustration, and sometimes even grief.

This is, of course, one of the principal ways we use relationships to create the pain of separation. Our parents, our siblings, our spouses and even our own children will oblige us by creating all sorts of disappointments in the form of broken promises or failures to perform in some way or another. Betrayal is another way in which we experience the pain of an unmet expectation, which in that case, would have been an expectation of trustworthiness.

For the purpose of this exercise, it will be helpful to look back at the expectations you might have held relative to each of your stories during the spiritual amnesia phase and to assess whether or not you were entitled to hold them. If not, then in order to dissolve that toxic energy, you can rescind them retrospectively.

After you have done that, it will be incumbent on you as an awakened individual, from that moment on, to look at any expectations you might have and ask yourself whether the expectation is realistic and whether you are actually entitled to hold it. In some cases, it will be appropriate, especially those which relate to your own boundaries and your value system. However, these need to be made explicit up front as requests and not just held as an unspoken expectation. Everyone needs to know where you and they stand.

I mentioned earlier in the book the issue over whether I was entitled to demand that my mother love me, and how that created some fierce discussion about entitlement and the presumption that love could and should be given. I then extended the discussion by asking the people to look at each of their victim stories and the associated suffering and then to ask themselves, "How did you want these people to be different to the way they were at that time? To what extent was that the main source of your pain? What were you demanding from them that you had no right to expect?" I would now like to put the same questions to you.

Exercise:
Look back at your own timeline and pick out the events where someone significant in your life did not measure up to your demand that they be a certain way or, in your eyes, let you down or disappointed you in some way. Write down all the expectations, demands, and judgments, and how you wanted that person to be or to change just to please you.

Love yourself for having these expectations because you know you created them for the same reason as you created the beliefs. Then, notwithstanding the fact that you wanted the disappointment in order to get some karmic units, evaluate from your new perspective, whether you had any right to expect the person to be different or whether you were being unrealistic in your demands.

When you do a Radical Forgiveness worksheet, you'll see a statement at Step #5 that goes like this:

"My discomfort was/is my signal that I am withholding love from myself and (X, the other person), by judging, holding expectations, wanting (X) to change and seeing (X) as less than perfect. *(List the judgments, expectations and behaviors that indicate that you wanted him/her/them to change.)"*

The idea here is to walk in the other person's shoes for a while and to understand where they are coming from. It also invites you to see, with due humility, that people are simply who they are, that you cannot change them and, indeed, have no right to expect them to be different. You can only change yourself or walk away if you need to.

It is also to give you the opportunity to stop making it all about you. You may be taking it all too personally. This exercise is rather challenging because it requires a lot of humility to back off from one's long-held demands and expectations that people be a certain way.

People who have a need to control have a very hard time letting go of expectations and their demands that people be different. As a consequence, they suffer a great deal during the spiritual amnesia phase. But once they are awake, they have to work hard to stop their controlling behavior—by loving themselves for being controlling!

Here are a few examples of some rather common demands that come up in my workshops, from people who are struggling to see how they are creating these circumstances within their relationships as a way to feel the pain of separation.

1. *My father wasn't there for me emotionally.*

2. *My sister/brother/nephew/grandchild didn't visit me.*

3. *My husband won't stop beating me.*

4. *My boss doesn't pay me enough and doesn't appreciate me.*

5. *My friend has cancer and needs us to send healing energy.*

Let's take each of these in turn and see what questions might arise in each case.

#1. *My father wasn't there for me emotionally.* This is a very common complaint grounded in the expectation that a father *should* be there emotionally for his daughter. But what right does a daughter have to expect that? Maybe he doesn't know how to be that way. Maybe he is consumed with his work and doesn't feel inclined much towards parenthood. Maybe he is not even aware of her need. Maybe he just isn't an emotional guy.

#2. *My sister/brother/nephew/grandchild didn't visit me.* I had a friend once who was very upset and angry that her nephew never came to visit her. After we did a Radical Forgiveness exercise, she said, *"I got it! He doesn't want to."* That was an epiphany for her, and it immediately brought her relief from her pain. She immediately dropped the expectation and demand that he should come to visit. I found out later that very soon after she had let go of her demand, he began to show up at her house. He didn't know that she had done anything, of course, but he must have felt her energy change and responded accordingly.

#3. *My husband won't stop beating me.* It's obviously reasonable that she demand her husband to stop beating her. However, once she wakes up to the fact that she wanted the abuse because she feels worthless or something like that, and she wants him to prove her right, then he will probably stop. If he doesn't,

224

then she needs to take action to make him stop, or leave. Forgiveness is not about being a doormat. As we have already discussed, it is essential that we have strong boundaries.

#4. *My boss doesn't pay me enough and doesn't appreciate me.* We might ask, "Have you asked your boss for more money? Perhaps he doesn't think you are worth more. If you were in his shoes, would you pay you more? Is it the going rate? Do you feel you don't deserve more? Can you go elsewhere?" Again, this might be a question of boundaries and personal empowerment once you have awakened.

#5. *My friend has cancer and needs us to send healing energy.* This is one that many people find challenging because, even though it is definitely rooted in victim consciousness, it doesn't seem like it. A lot of people fall into this trap. Unless the person has specifically asked for healing energy to be sent to him, it would be an arrogant assumption on your part to imagine that he actually wants it or needs it. What you would, in fact, be sending him is your judgment that his cancer experience is not OK. Who are we to say that he should not have cancer? To see someone in need of healing is to see them as less than perfect. This says more about our need to see victims everywhere than anything else.

An awakened person would simply send someone who is 'cancering' unconditional love and support and, even if he had asked for healing energy, would send prayers that he receive whatever outcome is the highest and best outcome for him to experience. Period. This is another way to practice expanding in Love.

What this brings us to, of course, is the realization that peace lies in our ability to love what is, just the way it is. We should, at least, start from that position, and then, if change is required, to go about creating the necessary change from that place of deep inner peace free from victim consciousness. As we saw in the previous chapter about beliefs, it is a paradox that the most effective way to bring about change of any kind is first to accept it totally just the way it is. This is often the best way to approach people. Trying to change people by coming from judgment about them is the least likely way to succeed in changing them. That includes trying to heal them.

However, this brings up some fundamental issues for people in the healing professions. How do they deal with this issue? This is especially poignant for doctors who deal with end of life issues or emergency situations where they have to make decisions on behalf of their patients. Their training requires them to always do everything possible to save lives, no matter what. Sometimes this means subjecting the patient to more suffering than if medical procedures were actually withheld. Seldom will doctors in a hospital (or family members come to that) allow someone to die with dignity. Death is always seen as failure and to be prevented at all costs. (This is expanded upon in Chapter 25: *Grieving Your Losses*.)

This being the case, it is up to us, as awakened human beings who are aware that death is an illusion, to take responsibility for our own manner of dying by writing out a Living Will that specifically defines how we shall be treated in particular circumstances.

But what about psychotherapists, life coaches and other such people in the 'helping' professions who are not dealing with life and death situations but are just trying to help people smooth out their lives and solve problems? The answer lies in how the conversation is initiated and which three questions they have in their mind as the client or patient walks through the door. If they work according to the standard medical model, they will have the following three questions in their head:

1. What's wrong with this person?
2. How did he/she get this way?
3. How can I fix this person?

When a therapist is coming from the new paradigm, the questions in their head (even though they may act in the beginning as if they were following the medical model) will be as follows:

1. What is occurring for this person that is perfect?
2. How is the perfection revealing itself?
3. How can I get the person to see the perfection in what is happening?

As you can see, it is a totally different mindset and a completely different way of looking at the person they are trying to help and the presenting problem (which in reality is not a problem). The process becomes less of a therapy and more a way of educating people. The goal is to get them to see the situation differently so they can simply dissolve the perceived problem using the Radical Living tools provided.

Exercise: List all the ways you want, or have wanted, someone to be different - no matter whether you think it is justified or not. Put down all your criticisms and judgments.

Person #1: *I think he/she should . . .* _____

_____

_____

_____

The objective is simply to notice them and to realize how much pain you have invested in your need for them to change. Then read the statement below to release the energy.

227

"I totally release my need for _____
to be different and free him/her to be who he/she is, without
judgment, and I hereby declare myself free to be in relationship with him/her or to leave if his/her way of being is too
toxic for me or just plain unacceptable. I am totally at choice
to do what is best for me. I am responsible only for myself."

Person #2: *I think he/she should* . . . _____

_____

_____

_____

"I totally release my need for _____
to be different and free him/her to be who he/she is, without
judgment, and I hereby declare myself free to be in relationship with him/her or to leave if his/her way of being is too
toxic for me or just plain unacceptable. I am totally at choice
to do what is best for me. I am responsible only for myself."

Person #3: *I think he/she should* . . . _____

_____

_____

_____

"I totally release my need for _____
to be different and free him/her to be who he/she is, without
judgment, and I hereby declare myself free to be in relationship with him/her or to leave if his/her way of being is too
toxic for me or just plain unacceptable. I am totally at choice
to do what is best for me. I am responsible only for myself."

21. Interpretations & Assumptions

Another thing you might need to do with each of your victim stories and your perpetrator stories is to look to see how much of the story is composed of the actual facts of what happened and how much of it is simply what you have made up, interpreted and assumed about what happened. As we mentioned earlier, in any one victim story, the pain surrounding the facts amounts to about 10% of the total emotional energy invested. The other 90% comes from 'awfulizing' it and adding in all the interpretations and assumptions. The 10% part is pain; the 90% part is suffering.

[If you didn't review this process while at page 213, you might wish to do so here. It is the dynamic that was initially referenced on Page 34. Go to www.ExpandinginLove.com or scan the code to watch it again.]

Example: "My husband had an affair." That's a fact which, in itself, will bring some pain, no doubt. But then come the interpretations that elevate the pain into suffering. "I am not enough for him." "I am not sexy enough." "All men cheat on me." "He doesn't love me." "There must be something wrong with me." Here are some more examples:

Fact: My father died.

Interpretations: He abandoned me. He died too soon. It was my fault. If I had cared more, he might have survived. He should have taken better care of himself. He wasted his life by taking too much risk. If he'd cared more about us, he wouldn't have put himself in such danger. He was selfish.

Fact: My mother divorced my Dad.

Interpretations: She took my father away from me. She broke up our family. She didn't try hard enough. He is the victim in this. She doesn't care that I don't have a father. It was all about her – what about me? It was my fault. They broke up because of me. If I hadn't come along before they were married, they wouldn't have gotten married at all.

Fact: My wife cheated on me.

Interpretations: Her boyfriend must be a better lover than me. She is a whore. I can never trust her again. I'm not good enough in bed for her. She needs to be punished. She didn't care about hurting me. She had no good reason to do it. She was cold-hearted and selfish. Her boyfriend is without scruples.

Fact: I was sexually abused by my father.

Interpretation: I must have deserved it. It was the only way I knew to get love from him. It was my fault. I couldn't say no. I was too frightened. No one would believe me. I can never trust men. All men will hurt me. I have to pack on the weight to make myself unattractive to men. Orgasm is wrong and bad.

The truth is, though, in each of these cases, we never were entitled to any of those interpretations. They invariably were just flat out wrong and in many ways quite stupid. And yet we defended them vigorously because they gave us the karmic units we needed. They added value to our victim story. But now we have awakened, we cannot go on defending them. We have to separate the assumptions and interpretations from the facts so we can come to peace about what actually happened.

Here's what the Radical Forgiveness worksheet says about this in Step #6:

> **I now realize that in order to feel the experience more deeply, my soul has encouraged me to create a BIGGER story out of the event or situation than it actually seemed to warrant, considering just the facts. This purpose having been served, I can now release the energy surrounding my story by separating the facts from the interpretations I have made up about it.** *(List the main interpretations and circle the level of emotion and attachment you have around each interpretation NOW.)*

Exercise:
1. Pick one or more of your stories where you can see that you've taken it personally and made it all about you, as well as having added lots of assumptions and interpretations. In your journal, make a list of the things that actually happened. Just the raw facts.

_____

_____

_____

_____

_____

_____

_____

_____

2. Then make a second list, noting down each and every interpretation, judgment and assessment you made about what happened, that is, everything that is, or was, made up by you.

_____

_____

_____

_____

_____

_____

_____

_____

_____

_____

_____

_____

_____

_____

_____

_____

_____

_____

22. Loving Your Projections

From a very early age, we learned to blame others for everything unpleasant that occurred, even when, in truth, we might have been responsible for it. While blaming is a good strategy for creating separation in relationship and works quite well, it is nothing compared to the mechanism of projection.

While blaming is done consciously and with awareness, projection is an entirely unconscious activity that is generated from deep down in our unconscious minds, wherein is stored a stinking heap of horrible, rotting emotional garbage. Generated originally as a result of having been shamed over something, it is pushed down and kept down there, out of sight and mind and away from the light, to ensure no one, least of all the owner, shall ever be acquainted with it again. It constitutes our self-loathing. It is composed of all the shameful qualities, thoughts, ideas, beliefs, perversions, instinctual drives and urges that we are deeply ashamed of and have denied, repressed and pushed out of our awareness altogether. Carl Jung named it our shadow.

The potential this shadow material offered for creating separation was enormous. First of all, it created separation within ourselves. It split us into two – the cool part and the uncool part – the half we presented to the world and the half we kept nicely hidden. Deep within ourselves, we created a terrible sense of non-self-acceptance and self-hatred of at least half of our beingness. Many of our core-negative beliefs arose out of this internal split and were the genesis of many of our victim/perpetrator stories.

It also offered endless opportunities to create separation between ourselves and others. This was achieved by subconsciously attracting into our lives others who seemed to exhibit some aspect of our own self-hatred. That enabled us then to subconsciously project that aspect onto them as a way to be rid of it and to make them into scapegoats. This is the mechanism of projection.

[To watch a video of me explaining projection with diagrams, scan the QR Code to go the website www.ExpandinginLove.com.]

By way of illustration, let's say someone came along who appeared to be very sure of himself and was obviously taking care to make sure his needs were met. But because he resonated our own deeply repressed judgments about how we always behave in our own self-interest, oftentimes to the severe detriment of others, we chose to perceive his behavior as 'selfishness.' That way, we could attack it 'out there' in him rather than face it within ourselves. With anger and self-righteous indignation, we heaped derision and heavy criticism on him for being so very selfish, never realizing that it was our own selfishness being reflected back to us. By doing that, we subconsciously kidded ourselves that we were cleansed of this aspect we so loathed in ourselves. That wasn't really the case; but by that time, we had created an enemy. Fait accompli!

But again, now that you have awakened and are dedicated to expanding in love, your immediate task is to undo this process of projection by recognizing that, as it says in #10 on the Radical Forgiveness Worksheet:

"I now realize that I get upset when someone resonates in me, something I have denied, repressed and projected onto them. I now see the truth in the adage, "If You Spot It, You Got It!" This person is reflecting what I need to love and accept in myself. I am now willing to take back the projection and own it as part of my shadow. I love and accept this part of me."

Once we recognize that what we see and criticize in others is simply a reflection of what we can't stand in ourselves, it becomes clear that we are being given an opportunity to heal the split within ourselves. By taking back all our projections and loving the parts of us we had previously hated, we expand into Love for ourselves and return ourselves to wholeness. We also expand our Love and gratitude for those who 'volunteered' to show up and mirror our shadow for us. Bear in mind, too, that this phenomena works with groups in exactly the same way as with individuals. It even works with countries. As we saw in Chapter 11, it was highly likely that America went to war with Iraq because Saddam Hussein resonated a huge amount of self-hatred and shame that was in America's shadow and he represented the perfect person and country on whom to project it.

Exercise:
Make a list of two people you have disliked and then list each and every quality you saw in them that you found unacceptable. Dig deep and be honest with yourself. Don't censor your list, even if you think you might be being unfair. Just tune into your own feelings of disapproval in regard to what you see.

Person 1.   Person 2.

_____   _____

_____   _____

_____   _____

_____   _____

235

Now here's the bit you're not going to like. Transfer each item on those two lists to the following worksheet.

THE EMBRACING MY SHADOW WORKSHEET

The qualities I am now seeing were being mirrored back to me by those people I found myself judging, and am willing to now love and accept as part of me, are:

_____

_____

_____

_____

_____

_____

_____

That sucks, doesn't it! Nevertheless, it is important to list every quality you saw in the two people and didn't like, even if some of them feel totally unlike you and, at first sight, you feel unable to own them. They may be highly symbolic of something in your shadow that is hard to identify, or be representative of some other quality that your subconscious mind links to the one listed, but several times removed.

The good news is that you don't have to know what these qualities symbolize or represent. It is simply a matter of accepting the principle, *"If You Spot It, You Got It."* In other words, if you see it in someone else and it upsets you, then it's yours. There are no exceptions to this rule.

236

The more what you see 'out there' upsets you, the more vital it is that you love and accept it within yourself. Resist the temptation to continue judging those qualities as 'bad' and criticizing yourself for having them. Doing that simply strengthens the shadow and increases your inner-directed shame. The only way to dissolve the energy it is to love it just the way it is. Also, just as we said that in order to take the power away from core-negative beliefs, it was essential to love ourselves for having the beliefs, it is every bit as important to love ourselves for having these qualities. They are who we are, at least for now. This is simply another way to expand into Love.

Subsequent Action
While looking at the list of qualities you have recognized as being the parts of you that you had previously denied, repressed and projected onto a lot of people, read the following statements out loud, slowly and deliberately, making sure you get the full meaning of the statement.

1. I now see that all these people have been mirroring for me the parts of myself I have made wrong and have judged, denied, repressed and projected onto them. I thank all of them for mirroring those parts of my shadow.

2. I am now taking back the projections and am now willing to love and accept this part of me. They each are a part of who I am, and I would not be complete without them.

3. I now realize they are not things to be overcome or gotten rid of. Neither are they obstacles standing in my way of my growth and healing. I love and accept each one just the way it is.

4. As I become willing to love and accept these parts of me, I trust that whatever caused me to form these shadow aspects, such as lies, misperceptions or the result of being shamed, will dissolve automatically as I come to love them.

5. *Conversely, I realize that if I continue to judge those parts of myself and resist loving them, they will grow stronger. (What you resist, persists.)*

6. *If the underlying belief about one or more is actually 'true,' then my acceptance of it as just being who I am will allow me to transform the energy and use the positive power inherent in that part of me to good purpose. (My perfection lies in my imperfection.)*

7. *Having brought my shadow aspects to the light, I realize that my Spiritual Intelligence has facilitated every one of these healing opportunities; and I honor and bless all the people on my list for being willing to be healing angels for me.*

Signed: _____

Date: _____

238

23. Reframing the Stories

Having looked at your beliefs, assumptions, interpretations and projections, all that is left for you to do now to retrieve your energy from the past, is to reduce your stories to rubble, one by one, by reframing them. Reframing our stories takes us to a completely new level, and it is nothing less than a giant step.

Reframing involves taking a story that was firmly rooted in victim consciousness and flipping it 180 degrees so it lands right in the center of the metaphysical paradigm we have been describing in this book. As soon as we do that, everything changes.

You may perhaps remember how we showed earlier that when you place a different frame around the same picture, the viewing experience is very different. It's the same with our stories. While the narrative doesn't change, our perception of it shifts when we change the frame.

The frame we have traditionally put around our accounts of what has befallen us in life contains the time-honored belief systems of victim consciousness. Here are some examples of what might be etched into the frame:

"It shouldn't have happened." "Someone is to blame." "Life is cruel, random, risky, dangerous and uncertain." "Life is a matter of chance, luck and coincidence." "You have to fight to survive." "It's a dog-eat-dog world." "Life is without meaning." "You are born, you live and you die." "Other people are responsible for my unhappiness." There are more, but you get the drift, I hope.

When we do a Radical Forgiveness reframe, we throw out all those old beliefs and assumptions. None of them have validity in the new paradigm we are shifting into. All of them are misperceptions, so we happily discard them and throw out the old frame.

Our new frame tells us that life is not like that at all. Life is meaningful, deliberate, divinely guided and purposeful. Life is full of wonderful synchronicities and meaningful connections. We are all One and spiritually connected. We create our reality, and we can have heaven on earth if we want it. Each one of us is responsible for our own happiness, and yet we also support each other with compassion and Love. There are no victims and no perpetrators. Everyone is getting what they want, and everything is in divine order. Death is not real. Love is the motivating force behind everything.

At first blush, you would think we are just playing mind games, simply exchanging one way of languaging for another, like it's some kind of trick or clever swap. That's certainly how it seems.

But for me, there has to be more to it than that because the kind of changes I see in people when they open up to the possibility that life can be viewed in this context are nothing short of extraordinary. And it's not just that they feel so much better, which they do, but their whole life changes dramatically as well. The other people involved in their story are affected too, even though they have not been involved in this process. And the situation that gave rise to the story in the first place gets magically resolved.

But it's not magic and it's not trickery. It's an energy phenomenon. I'm sure the quantum physicists could give us a scientific explanation in these terms. But my observations, based as they are on 20 years of experience, confirm that as soon as we become willing to entertain this possibility, not only does the energy field around the story change, but the entire situation changes. And the effect is immediate, no matter the distances involved, so obviously time and space do not apply. That shows that it can only be energy.

Rupert Sheldrake has shown that if one person within a morphogenetic field changes their energy, everyone else in the field is affected in some way. If it is a strong shift of energy, it will have a correspondingly strong effect all through that field. Interestingly, it makes no difference if the family is dispersed all over the globe. Energetically, they are still connected. *(Go back to Page 74 and scan the QR code to review the video on this.)*

We all belong to other fields such as work groups, special interest groups and so on. But the group we are interested in here would be composed of all the people who have played a part in your story. Besides the person who victimized you, there may be supporters of that person, your own family members, lawyers, police, insurance agents, bankers, therapists and others. All together, they would constitute a morphogenetic field, which means they are all energetically connected in a very dynamic way.

When you go through the process of reframing the situation, it has the effect changing the energy flow within that morphogenetic field, and everyone feels it. And because the underlying energy that is sourcing the reframe is Love, the result will always be positive or, shall we say, to the highest and best for those concerned.

How to Write a Reframe
Because it depends on the new paradigm in which we are not yet fully grounded, people do have difficulty coming up with the right

words and the right feel for a reframe. Since it is the step that facilitates the shift from victim consciousness to a Love consciousness, it is important to get the right feeling into it in order that the transition is properly experienced.

The way you reframe your situation should allow you to feel its perfection from the spiritual standpoint and to become aware of the Grace inherent in it. Your reframe should offer a way of looking at your situation that reveals the hand of God or Divine Intelligence working for you and showing you how much It loves you. However, it need not be overly complicated. The reframe might simply be expressed in a very general way, such as:

"What happened was simply the unfoldment of a divine plan and was meant to happen that way, not TO me, but FOR me. It was called forth by my own Higher Self for my spiritual growth, and the people involved were doing a healing dance with me; so, in truth, nothing wrong ever happened."

Writing something like that would be perfectly adequate. On the other hand, if you add some details about the situation, that would be fine too.

What would NOT be appropriate would be to write an interpretation based on assumptions rooted in the World of Humanity, like giving reasons why it happened, making excuses or saying what you got out of it.

In spite of this warning, I found that a lot of people still seemed to want to write about the benefits they obtained as if that were the point of the experience. They were generally having trouble writing a spiritual reframe that expressed the essence of the new paradigm. For that reason, I wrote the following essay and put it on my blog. I hope you will find it helpful.

Blog Entry, August, 2007

The idea that everything is unfolding according to a Divine plan so there is nothing to forgive—which is the essence of *Radical Forgiveness*—is difficult to ground in everyday reality. That's why we have created a number of tools that help us to express the willingness to be open to that possibility which, fortunately for us, is all that is required for the process to work.

However, the RF tools invite us to 'see the perfection' in the situation and, in some cases, actually ask us to come up with a specific reframe. People find this to be the most difficult thing to get right in the *Radical Forgiveness* process, so this essay is devoted to clarifying what might count as an appropriate reframe and what wouldn't.

Inherent in the RF process is the notion that we are not trying to change anything in the outer world; rather we are simply trying to change our minds about it. Let me make it clear, however, that we are not creating anything that is actually true. We are just exchanging one story for another; one interpretation for another; one paradigm for another.

When we reframe a situation, we exchange one set of assumptions rooted in the world of humanity for another set rooted in the unseen and essentially mysterious world of Spirit. It is not the veracity of the story that matters; rather it is how we frame it with assumptions anchored in the World of Spirit that becomes the test as to whether it is indeed a *Radical Forgiveness* reframe or not.

It is very common for people, even seasoned *Radical Forgiveness* coaches and graduates, to express their reframes in terms of having received a 'gift,' a 'lesson' or even a 'healing' that remains, to all intents and purposes, firmly anchored in the World of Humanity, even though they are dressed up in spiritual language. They nevertheless fail the test.

During a conversation with a very good friend of mine, who was herself a holocaust survivor, she told me about an exhibition in the Holocaust Museum in Auschwitz, Germany, that featured a huge pile of children's shoes. All of them had been taken from the children before they were gassed. As you would expect, the exhibit has an extremely visceral and profound effect on anyone who confronts it.

As a student of *Radical Forgiveness,* she made an attempt to reframe it, primarily so she could come to terms with it herself and integrate it somehow into her own personal history of having been part of that terrible experience. She said that perhaps the reframe was that the 'gift' (there's that word again — always a trap), was that the souls of the children 'volunteered' to die in this way so that people who saw the pile of shoes would ensure that, since children are always the victims of war, they would never create war again. In that sense, there was a Divine purpose in what happened.

In that statement were indeed two assumptions rooted in the World of Spirit. One was that there is no death and souls choose when and how to make their transition both in and out of human form. The second was that there was Divine purpose even in this situation. It counts, perhaps, as a partial reframe to that extent. But making it about "stopping wars" snapped it right back into the World of Humanity. It, therefore, failed the test. It was not a true *Radical Forgiveness* reframe. Even if such a result was to occur, which it never would because it doesn't get to the root of why humans kill each other, it would simply be an "effect," not a reframe. It would be simple cause and effect, which only operates in the World of Humanity, not in the World of Spirit.

My reframe of the shoes story, even though I haven't seen the exhibit, and it might well be different afterwards, might run something like this: "The souls who inhabited those children's bodies incarnated with a specific mission to be killed in a particularly gruesome manner to teach us that we are all One, that separation is not real, that death is not real and that when we senselessly kill a seemingly innocent child, we kill ourselves. And that we are all children of God; the One 'Sonship.'"

It might also be part of a larger reframe which I have spoken of publicly in the past and have held seminars on: that the soul lesson inherent in the Holocaust was about our letting go of 'victim consciousness' which the Jewish people volunteered to exhibit to the extreme. It was also about the error of 'specialness' that the Germans volunteered to demonstrate to an equal extreme. The only meaningful opposite of victimhood and specialness is Oneness.

In anticipation of someone asserting that the reframe inherent in Jill's Story (Chapter One in my book *Radical Forgiveness*) fails the test because I made it about saving my sister's marriage and 'healing' her core-negative belief that her father didn't love her, let me say this. If it were just about that, it would fail the test. What it was really about, though, and Jill really did get this, was that her own Spiritual Intelligence created the whole scenario as an opportunity to learn that she was loved, she was whole and complete with or without a man, and she was entirely responsible for her life and that only Spirit is real. The rest was simply an illusion — a victim story based in the World of Humanity which she was able to release.

I hope this helps you in the process of doing a *Radical Forgiveness* worksheet, in particular with Step number 18. Having said all this, it really doesn't matter what you write on

245

the worksheet. Your intention to do it is enough. You cannot screw it up! Would God care if you failed the reframe test? I don't think so.

Languaging

Another thing I have found to be helpful in finding the right languaging for a reframe is this list of statements, which are quite close to those that form the content of the 13 Steps to Radical Forgiveness audio process. It's fine to use some selected phrases from any of these questions to create a reframe. (In some cases, there is a number reference to a similar question on the RF Worksheet.)

1. Even though I may not understand why, I am willing to recognize that my soul has created this situation for my spiritual growth. And that, in that sense, I was, in fact, getting exactly what I unconsciously wanted from (X). [RFW # 12]

2. I am willing to entertain the possibility that I asked (X) to give me this experience in order to experience separation. [RFW # 8]

3. I am now able to see that this situation is giving me an opportunity to heal the misperception that I am separate and alone.

4. I am, therefore, ready and willing to cancel my contract with (X) and to let go of my unconscious need to stay a victim.

5. I am willing to release my need to judge the situation as right or wrong, good or bad. Even though I cannot explain how or why, I am willing to allow the situation to be perfect just the way it is. [RFW #13]

6. I am willing to be open to the idea that this person is helping me reconnect with my true nature and access the power within me.

7. I now recognize that in forgiving him/her, I have forgiven myself.

8. I am now able to release the need to blame and to be right about this, and I am *WILLING* to see the perfection in the situation just the way it is. [RFW # 13]

9. I now realize that (X) was playing out a role for me and that we were each playing out our parts of the soul contract we made before incarnating. Therefore, it was all perfect and there is nothing to forgive. **10.** I let go of my need to make (X) responsible for my unhappiness.

11. I recognize that in withholding love from (X) *(by judging)*, I was withholding love from myself and you, (X). I release you, (X), to be as God created you and give up my expectations and need that you be any different. [RFW #5]

12. Instead of living in the victim's question - *WHY?* - I now choose to live in the question of what the **blessing** might be for me in having (X) in my life.

Exercise:
1. Revisit each story and write a thoughtful reframe for each one. For a preamble to get you started, we need look no further than what you are invited to say in Step 16 on the Radical Forgiveness worksheet.

16. I now realize that what I was experiencing (my victim story) was a precise reflection of my limited, "world-of-humanity" perception of the situation. I now understand that I can change this 'reality' by simply being willing to see the spiritual "big-picture" perfection in the situation. For example........

2. After having completed all the reframes, written in a notebook or journal perhaps, read out loud the following statements, taken from the worksheet:

17. I completely forgive myself, (YOUR NAME), and accept myself as a loving, generous and creative being. I release all need to hold onto emotions and ideas of lack and limitation connected to the past. I withdraw my energy from the past and release all barriers against the love and abundance that I know I have in this moment. I create my life and I am empowered to be myself again, to unconditionally love and support myself, just the way I am, in all my power and magnificence.

18. I now SURRENDER to the Higher Power I think of as _____, and trust in the knowledge that this situation will continue to unfold perfectly, and in accordance with Divine guidance and spiritual law. I acknowledge my Oneness and feel myself totally reconnected with my Source. I am restored to my true nature, which is LOVE, and I now restore love to (X). I close my eyes in order to feel the LOVE that flows in my life, and to feel the joy that comes when the love is felt and expressed.

3. Spend at least two minutes in meditation tuning into to that joy and the Love.

24. Writing Three Letters

I have come to believe that there is no better way to dissolve the energy of a grievance as a way to expand into Love than by writing these three letters in the manner I am about to describe. This is especially true if there is a lot of energy and pain attached to the story. The letters you write are each written from a very different mind-set and exhibit a very different energy in each case, so I advise that you to allow 24 hours to elapse between each one.

Doing the Radical Forgiveness worksheet certainly has the same effect on you as doing these three letters, but we have found that doing these seem to open the heart more. The second letter in particular promotes more compassion, empathy and understanding which is why this process offers a greater opportunity to expand into Love than a worksheet might. This is why I would normally suggest to someone whose grievance is with a 'love partner,' past or present, to use this particular tool.

While it certainly works really well when you are really upset about something that has just happened, it will work just as well on something that may have happened a long time ago, even if the person is dead or nowhere around. Remember, you are doing this for yourself in order to expand into Love, not for the other person. And in any case, you would never tell the people you are forgiving them. They do not need to know, and you should have no need to tell them. If you do feel that need, then look at your need to control or manipulate the other person (because that's what telling them that you have forgiven them would amount to). They will know anyway, energetically, that something has changed between you because, as we saw in the last chapter, they are connected to you energetically.

Note: None of the three letters that you write in this process should ever be sent.

Letter #1

This letter is the easiest to write because, in essence, it is your victim story. You have probably gone over it in your mind a thousand times, so once you start writing, it will all come pouring out in a torrent of accusatory and even vengeful language. That is, so long as you don't censor it in any way. Just let it rip, and let the person know just how much he/she has hurt you, wounded you, damaged you and so on. You make no excuses for the person and show no mercy whatsoever. All you know is that you are the victim in this situation. Vent all your anger and rage in this letter. Hold nothing back. You can threaten vengeance of the vilest kind if it makes you feel good. Keep writing until you have nothing left to say. Get everything out. It might take many pages.

The process of writing this letter may cause you to shed a lot of tears – tears of rage, sadness, resentment and hurt. Let them flow. Have a box of tissues beside you. If you are angry, scream into a pillow or do some physical activity to help you feel your anger. *Remember, under no circumstances are you to mail this letter!*

Letter #2

This is a much more difficult letter to write and requires you to be in a more reflective frame of mind, which, as I have already said, it best done the next day after you have cooled down somewhat and slept on it. It allows a dream cycle to occur between each letter so each one can be processed by the subconscious mind. That said, don't go more than two days between writing the first and second letter.

Whereas the first letter expresses the raw victim story this second one is where you reduce the amount of energy invested in the story by coming to the realization that while your pain is in what actually happened, the suffering is in how you expanded the story with a whole slew of erroneous interpretations, assumptions, unmet expectations and so on.

This letter, therefore, should help you sort out what is or was true versus what you imagined was true. In that sense, this part of this letter might become something of a dialogue with yourself about what happened as if you were musing about the whole thing, trying to make some sense of it, stripping out and noting down everything you made up about the story that was just not true.

Letting go of what may have given you more self-righteous "juice" in your story takes a lot of humility and courage. You may also come to realize in this letter that how you expanded your story is a reflection of a pattern in which you repeatedly apply a set of old beliefs about yourself and life. You may have held these beliefs for a long time and they might have shown up many times before.

The second part of Letter #2 is going to resemble what we would normally expect to be the sentiment expressed with the best of traditional forgiveness. It is still firmly based in victim consciousness in that you don't let the person off the hook for having committed the crime, but it does ask you to be more conciliatory, understanding and empathetic and to cut the person some slack. It also asks that you put yourself in the other person's shoes and imagine whether you might have done the same had you been in a similar circumstance or frame of mind.

You might need to take into account their upbringing and life experiences. For example, people who have themselves been wounded are likely to act out their repressed rage on someone else. People who abuse children are nearly always people who were themselves abused as children. People who were abandoned as children are likely to abandon others later in life. The task in this letter, then, is to do your best to bring humility, tolerance, understanding and compassion to the situation — even if at this time you are not actually feeling it. Let me give you an example out of my own experience.

My first wife, Jean (now deceased), and I had been married six years; and at that time, I was studying full-time for my degree at University. During my summer vacation, I agreed to be at home and take care of our three children while she went back to work for the duration. She was missing that lifestyle. Well, she fell in love with a guy and, I came to find out later, had sex with him on our seventh wedding anniversary. As you can imagine, I was furious and played the victim up to the hilt.

Months later, when we were able to have a sensible discussion about the whole episode, I came to understand what had happened and began to see it from her point of view. It turned out that she became totally and irrationally besotted by this man. Needless to say, he was married and had no intentions of taking it further. She was in such pain, I began to forget my own pain and started to feel compassion for her. She was not promiscuous or irresponsible, so the fact that this had happened was something out of the ordinary for her, to say the least. In retrospect, she realized the guy just used her for a little extramarital sex on the side, but she didn't see it that way at the time. She had fantasized all sorts of scenarios with him.

What I came to understand was that she was literally out of her mind with what she thought at the time was love. She had absolutely zero control over her emotions and was being totally controlled by them. She was completely bowled over by him, and I realized that there was nothing that she could have done about it. When it was all over and she returned to her senses and saw how close she had come to ruining her life and hurting her children, she was devastated and deeply ashamed.

As I said, I started out angry, hurt and victimized, but as I came to see what had actually happened as opposed to how I thought it had happened, I began to feel sorry for her because of the pain she suffered as a consequence.

While I was all tied up in Victimland about what had happened, I had made it up that it was all about me and the kids. I had made up a story in my mind about how she must have done it just to hurt me and punish me for all that was not good in the marriage. I blamed her for everything and made her wrong as a wife and a mother. I expanded the story in my mind and imagined all sorts of things that never actually happened. I beat myself up for being a weak and feckless husband, otherwise why else would she have gone 'looking out' for someone else. I made it up that I was sexually inadequate, especially when she told me that the only time she felt satisfied was with him. I felt like a sexual cripple and felt certain that I would never be able to satisfy a woman.

Here's how I might have written my second letter to her:

Dear Jean,

I am still feeling a lot of pain and hurt about the fact that you cheated on me and had an affair with a married man, especially that you had sex with him on our wedding anniversary which really hurt. I felt very betrayed, and I couldn't help thinking that you did it to punish me.

But since our conversation, I am now realizing that you didn't do it out of any malice toward me and had no intention whatsoever to go out and find someone to have an affair with, even though I said you did. I know that is not you, and it is not in your nature to be cruel and inconsiderate.

I realize now that I took on a lot of negative feelings about myself that I blamed you for creating, but I know now they are not really true. I can see that you were totally controlled by your feelings and were unable to think clearly or rationalize what you were doing and that your feelings were so intense that you were more or less temporarily out of your mind. The very fact that you admitted you were so irrational that you would have left the kids and gone with him tells me that. That is so out of character for you because you are so devoted to our kids.

But it was also beyond your own previous experience to have such an intense emotional experience, and I can, therefore, understand how it would have knocked you off your feet and created such turmoil in you that you hardly knew what reality was. You were in such a state of confusion, poor thing. It must have been terrible for you in spite of the moments of ecstasy. And then when he took off and left you with nothing but your guilt and shame, that must have been awful.

But you must also see how much it hurt me and made me feel worthless and no good. I need you to take responsibility for that because the fact is you did what you did and it was a betrayal, no matter how you justify it. I am willing to take you back into my life, but I don't know that I could ever trust you again. How could I ever trust you after what you did?

Colin

Letter #3

While the first two letters were expressions of your authentic thoughts and feelings, this third letter will not be. It will be a 'fake-it-till you-make-it,' attempt at a reframe. You write it as if you believed it totally, with as much fervor and skill as you did with the previous two letters, even though with this one, you feel as if you are a fraud. It doesn't matter; your body will get it.

In this letter, you attempt to describe a new interpretation of the situation based on the principles of Radical Forgiveness. In other words, you write that you now realize that the person was, at the soul level, acting out of love by doing what he/she did because it was what you (your soul) wanted to experience. You had, in fact, recruited him/her to do it, not TO you, but FOR you.

It is even likely that you and the other person had agreed up front, prior to incarnation, that he/she would provide this experience for you — a soul contract in other words. All you are now able to feel towards this person is gratitude. You can use all the resources contained in the previous chapter to get this letter written, but by way of an example, let me indicate how I might have written my third letter to my ex-wife.

Dear Jean,

I now realize that you and I were doing a divine dance together as two souls supporting each other in the fulfillment of our desire to experience the pain of separation in a variety of forms. In sharing so much about how you felt badly rejected and betrayed by the man you were in love with, and the guilt and shame you felt subsequently about betraying me, I can only imagine that those were the emotional qualities that you had chosen to experience at that particular time in your life.

I realize that you made that choice probably before we incarnated and that I, as a member of your soul group, agreed to be the one who would get hurt. This was not just to help you, I hasten to add. My soul wanted to have the experience of being humiliated and betrayed, so I enrolled your soul to provide that opportunity for my spiritual growth and soul's evolution.

So, it was clearly a mutually beneficial agreement, and you and I played it out to perfection. We were healing angels for each other. It was early on in my incarnation, and I was extremely insecure about my sexuality and very vulnerable, so your timing was impeccable. It took me to exactly where my soul wanted to go — into the awful pain of jealousy, anger, resentment, sadness and shame.

The experience you gave me accelerated my healing and growth which in turn enabled me to develop the work I am doing now in this lifetime rather than in a future one. I am now clear that you did nothing wrong and that it was all part of a divine plan.

I am very grateful for what you were willing to do for me, especially since it caused you a lot of pain and anguish at the human level of experience. You were a blessing in my life at that time. Having completed the agreement we made before incarnating, it became clear to us both that the purpose for our relationship was essentially fulfilled and that it was time to move on. Our children had chosen us as their parents, knowing that this was our contract and that this would provide one of their challenges too. So, it was perfect that we should separate at that time and move in different directions. You chose cancer as a way to transition from this vibration into the Oneness which I am certain you are now experiencing to the fullest extent possible, having been given the gift of experiencing its opposite. My soul looks forward to connecting with you again in that world.

Love, Colin

Refer back to the previous chapter and utilize some of that suggested language for a reframe.

The result will be that you will feel a whole lot better for doing these three letters; and if the situation is still ongoing, it will probably resolve itself fairly quickly thereafter.

Self-Forgiveness

You can also do the same thing for Radical SELF-Forgiveness. You simply write the same three letters to yourself. You might find it helpful to do this since it is often the case that in going through the process of forgiving someone, you get in touch with some guilt and shame about how it might have been, at least in part, as much your fault as theirs.

Basically what you do is write the first letter from a self-confessed perpetrator's standpoint, lambasting yourself for what you have done. Guess whose services you will ask for in order to help you write this letter? Of course, your Inner Judging Self. He or she will relish the task and will launch a tirade of criticism against you, trying hard to make you feel as guilty as possible. It will feel as if you are channeling your Judging Self when writing this letter.

In the second letter, you will retire the Judging Self to some degree and switch to channeling your Self-Loving Self. It will provide some counterpoint to your Judging Self's strident criticism by bringing some compassion and understanding to your situation, sufficient at least to reduce the level of guilt and shame within you and for you to feel accepted.

In the third letter, which is the reframe, you write to your Higher Self, saying how you see that what you did was meant to happen for whatever reason and that you realize that there is nothing for which you need to be forgiven at the spiritual level. Your Higher Self will always say 'yes' because it knows the truth.

As I indicated earlier, Radical Forgiveness is a 'fake-it-till-you-make-it' process, and it is no less so with Radical Self-Forgiveness. In both cases, the first letter is easy to write because that will most likely reflect your state of mind at the time. Writing the second letter, though, is much harder to do. You have to try really hard to find true compassion and understanding for the perpetrator, or for yourself if you are doing the self-forgiveness. You may well have to fake a lot of the second letter, but don't worry; it is still working at the subconscious level.

But when it comes to writing the third letter, unless you have integrated the Radical Forgiveness philosophy into your everyday consciousness, you will almost certainly have to fake it. But again, that's OK. Your Spiritual Intelligence gets it. That's why you feel better almost immediately, no matter how skeptical you were while writing it.

25. Getting Yourself off the Hook

If any of those stories packed away in boxes up there in the attic turn out to have had some feelings of guilt and shame attached them, they may well be screaming out for some self-forgiveness on your part. Make this a priority.

Guilt and shame are very effective in creating separation. However, since they are both very toxic emotions and carry a low vibration, you will need to transform those energies as soon after awakening as possible. So, let's first define them so we know what we are dealing with.

Guilt is remorse over something you have done, or should have done but didn't. Shame is remorse over who you think you are. They are different but often connected. "I feel guilty because I did this, but I am ashamed of myself for doing it and am a very bad person."

Everyone agrees that forgiving oneself is much more difficult than forgiving others. In fact, even when you have forgiven someone 'out there,' there is an ever-present danger you will become tempted to turn it inwards and project it all back on yourself. It's a remnant of the old paradigm that we feel that someone must be blamed for what happened. If it's not their fault, then it must be ours.

The key to understanding how these energies are transformed is in knowing to which part of ourselves we are making the appeal for forgiveness. When we are forgiving others, it is easy to see that we are the forgiver and the other person is the one being forgiven.

However, when we try to forgive ourselves, we are trying to be both the forgiver and the forgiven at the same time. Judge, jury and witness all in the same case. The problem is further compounded by the fact that we are not one single self. We are a whole community of selves, all of whom have their own perspective on the matter. The key players in the matter of self-forgiveness are the inner judge and critical parent. I'm sure you are familiar with these two characters. The inner judge is the one that is always telling you that you are guilty and should be punished, while the critical parent never misses an opportunity to shame you in some way. Both are programmed never to grant you self-forgiveness.

With these two characters in charge, there's no chance. That's why conventional self-forgiveness can never work. The inner judge and critical parent have the veto. Other characters may fight for you and try to get some compassion going on your behalf, but nothing can get past those two 'nasties.' The answer is always 'NO.'

So, we must look elsewhere for the solution. If the odds are stacked against you in that court of appeal, stop going there. Take your appeal to a different court and an alternative presiding judge, one who loves you, understands you completely and will always say 'Yes' whenever you ask for forgiveness. That one is your *Higher Self.* It's not that it is more benevolent or just a sentimental pushover. No. It will say 'Yes' because it knows who you are, why you are here and what you are here to do. And it understands that you have never in your whole life done anything wrong or made one single mistake. That means there's nothing to forgive yourself for. Period.

The way to make that appeal to the Higher Self is to brief the part of yourself that has direct access to that Self – your Spiritual Intelligence. To do this is easy. All you need to do is write up a Self-Forgiveness worksheet (the brief) and let your Spiritual Intelligence take care of the rest. It's just like having your own internal barrister with direct access to the highest judge in the land.

Exercise:
1. In your Journal, make a list of all those things for which you feel you might have some self-forgiveness to do. What were you blaming yourself for? What have you judged yourself for? Where have you been "should-ing" on yourself? What was the content of your self-talk? What has your inner critic been saying to you?

2. Look first at the situation in human terms, and decide if your guilt was appropriate or inappropriate. In other words, ask yourself if you were you entitled to feel guilty, or did you take on the guilt when it was neither your fault nor your responsibility?

For example, suppose you were a factory owner but were very slack about health and safety. A worker injured himself seriously because the machine he was working on was not properly guarded. Should you feel guilty? Yes, of course. However, if you had done everything possible to make that machine safe, but the worker had chosen to remove the guard in order to increase his output, since he was paid on the number produced, are you then entitled to feel guilty? No. This is obviously a very clear case, but often it is not so clear; and it's worth taking some time to apply some careful thought to each situation.

3. Now read the following statements out loud and mark
AGREE or DON'T AGREE.

1. Even though I don't understand how or why, I am willing to be open to the possibility that the situation may have been purposeful – and that my Higher Self created the situation for my spiritual growth.

AGREE/DON'T AGREE

2. I now realize that my upset is a direct reflection of something that needed to be healed and that, even though I may not be seeing it yet, the healing message is contained in the situation.

AGREE/DON'T AGREE

3. Even though I am responsible and accountable for my actions in the World of Humanity, I am nevertheless willing to give up my need to judge myself or my action as right or wrong, good or bad. Even if I cannot explain how or why, I am willing to allow the situation to be just the way it is without attaching a judgment to it.

AGREE/DON'T AGREE

4. I am open to the idea that the way that I have been, the way I am now and all that I have done or are doing currently is totally purposeful in the grand scheme of things, and that what I judge about myself might be exactly what is called for in the Divine Plan – even to the extent that I am, or was, quite possibly a healing angel for someone.

AGREE/DON'T AGREE

5. Even though I have no idea at all how I might have been playing a healing angel for someone, or who that might have been, I am willing to accept – and feel, right here in this moment – their profound appreciation over my being prepared to do this for them – and at such discomfort to myself.

AGREE/DON'T AGREE

6. I am willing to be open to the idea that I attracted them into my life and that, subconsciously, we had both been receiving exactly what we both have needed – enabling each of us to let go of our addiction to being a victim.

AGREE/DON'T AGREE

7. I am now willing to acknowledge myself and appreciate myself for doing this thing and, in turn, to thank whoever is doing the dance with me, and for being a healing angel for me.

AGREE/DON'T AGREE

8. I now recognize that in being willing to see the perfection in the situation, I have now, in fact, forgiven myself and the other person.

AGREE/DON'T AGREE

NOTE: These statements are extracted from the audio process entitled, *'The 13 Steps to Radical SELF-Forgiveness.'* T The 13 Steps to Radical Self-Forgiveness is also available on CD from the E-Store.

[This 13-Step Process, and all the other 13-Step Processes available on the membership site, are many times more powerful as a listening experience rather than just reading it as you have just done here. Scan the QR code to go to www.radicalforgiveness.com/member, to access these tools.]

 To listen to a beautiful song by Karen Taylor-Good that will nicely round out this chapter, scan the QR Code to go to www.ExpandinginLove.com. It's called "I Forgive You — Me." You will love it!

263

26. Grieve Your Losses

There is probably no greater pain of separation than that which we feel at the death of a loved one. We suffer it even more intensely if the death itself is untimely, unexpected or tragic. It is not always about losing people either. The death of a pet can be equally traumatic for many of us.

Not that we don't suffer grief over other things as well, of course, like the loss of a job, a house, a relationship, a preferred way of life, our freedom (as when imprisoned), and so on. Nevertheless, while the process of dealing with grief is more or less the same no matter what the loss is, it surely remains true that the pain we feel over the death of a loved one is likely to be the most intense form of grief we are ever likely to feel.

While most of us in our lives experience this form of separation pain, we do not, in western cultures at least, allow ourselves to grieve to the extent that we might, given the intensity of the suffering that a death can cause. Whereas in other cultures, people observe a number of quite elaborate rituals and set aside quite long periods of time for grieving, we are expected to suppress the pain, be over it in a few days and be back at work as soon as possible.

It is likely, therefore, that most people could revisit their loss with a view to completing the grieving process and find it most beneficial. This is especially true if some forgiveness is required as well, which is often the case. Again, it is part of our attitude toward death to always think that it shouldn't have happened or that when it does, someone must have failed or was to blame for it in some way.

This is why doctors in America have to pay enormous sums of money for insurance against being sued when someone in their care dies, and why the cost of medical care in the last few months of life accounts for around 85% of all medical costs. Families insist that the doctors do everything possible to keep the person alive, no matter the cost and no matter how little quality of life will remain. Anything but death. And when it does occur, they want to blame someone and hold them responsible for the pain.

It is also not uncommon to make the person who died responsible for the pain. Death is the ultimate abandonment, and we feel it as such. Children who lose a parent often feel it as an abandonment and can never forgive the parent for dying and leaving them.

Exercise
Make a list of all the incidents in your life where death separated you from someone who was important to you.

1. On a scale of 1 - 10, estimate how much grief you felt (or feel) over losing this person. 1 = hardly any at all, and 10 = Intense grief and suffering.

2. Who do you blame or hold responsible for the person's death?

3. What feelings did you have immediately following the death?

4. What feelings do you have now?

This will naturally vary according to the circumstances of the death. For example, if your mother died peacefully at age 95 after a long and happy life and was starting to get ill, your grief will be of a different order than if she died relatively young, having been killed by a hit-and-run driver. Parents who lose a child suffer a lot because for a child to predecease its own parents seems out of the natural order of things.

Radical Grieving
So what does Radical Grieving, as one of the Tipping Method Strategies, have to offer that is different? Well, having by this time reached this place in the book, you will probably be able to imagine what this system of grieving has to offer that will qualify it as radical. Have you not already listed other forms of pain and suffering in the context of the new paradigm, including the assumption that everything that happens is all part of the divine plan? So, why not death?

The Stages of Grief
The most common approach to grieving, with which you might be familiar, is to help people go through the five stages of grief. They vary somewhat but basically follow this format:

1. Shock and denial
2. Anger
3. Depression
4. Bargaining
5. Acceptance

Elizabeth Kubler-Ross is the one everyone thinks of as having created this taxonomy of grief, but apparently she was misquoted. Her stages weren't about grieving so much as about the stages cancer patients tend to go through during the dying process. Nevertheless, it did form the basis for the idea that when we lose someone, we do stagger along some kind of looping, winding

267

pathway beginning with shock and denial and ending in final acceptance and release.

Most books and online programs focus on that approach; and if you want to research this further, just Google 'stages of grief,' and you will find plenty of resources available to you. But what I want to focus on is how we might deal with grief from the perspective of Radical Grieving.

It probably won't surprise you to realize that the Radical Grieving process follows more or less the same five stages which characterize Radical Forgiveness: telling the story, feeling the feelings, collapsing the story, reframing the story and integrating the new story. Additionally, there is some limited correlation between these five stages and the normal stages of grief, albeit only at the beginning.

The first three stages of Radical Forgiveness correlate to the commonly described stages of grief: shock (telling the story); anger and depression (feeling the feelings); and some of the bargaining (collapsing the story).

But let me say right here and now, I totally support the notion that we should allow ourselves to feel all the feelings and to feel them fully. Grief, anger, rage, disappointment, loneliness, sadness, guilt and any other feeling that might be included.

Radical Grieving is not a way to short circuit our grief. It is a way to transform it. But it cannot be transformed if we don't allow ourselves to feel the pain in the first place. So, yes, we need to feel the anger, the depression, the guilt, the sadness and the rage for as long as we need to in order to get that energy moving. Only then can we move into the transformation of those feelings.

But where the correlation between the normal 5-stage approach to grieving and Radical Grieving comes to an end is in how we complete the bargaining and come to the place of acceptance. The 5-Stage approach to death references the old paradigm and assumes that #5, 'acceptance,' is about coming to terms with everything according to how things operate according to that (old) world view. Even though we come to a place of acceptance and are able to move on, we still feel 'bad' that it happened, simply because it happened. This is separate from the pain we feel because we miss them. (This distinction will be discussed in a moment.)

The fourth and fifth stages of the Radical Forgiveness process – reframing the story and integrating the new story are, on the other hand, grounded in the new paradigm. As you know, this asks us to be open to the idea that there are no accidents or mistakes and that everything that happens is exactly how it is meant to be. This includes the manner and timing of our death if we make the assumption that, as souls, we choose and create all the experiences of our lives. Even death by murder, if it were to happen, would be included because we would have to assume our soul wanted that experience.

I am writing this at the very moment that the world is reliving the great crime of 9/11, ten years after to the day. I have to admit, when I see it all again on the TV screen, I find it all the more difficult to buy into this new paradigm. But even so, while we may have a lot of Radical Forgiveness to do on the perpetrators of such a crime, we have to ask ourselves whether we are really entitled to say that it should not have happened if that was the wish of the 3,000 souls who died at that time and in that manner. And what about the family members left behind? Might it not have been their soul's wish to experience the pain of separation that way? And what about the soul-wish of humanity itself? Who's to say that we didn't all choose to participate in the event in the hope that some, yet to be realized, good would come from it? In the days following 9/11, when Congress met to pay its respects, the chaplain was heard to say, "The hand of God was in there somewhere." I believe he meant it was our destiny and that good would someday emerge and cleanse the appearance of evil.

Radical Grieving, then, is very much akin to Radical Forgiveness and is just as much an affront to our normal way of thinking and strong beliefs. But as you know, the caveat we always add to it is that we don't have to believe any of it. We only have to be willing to be open to the idea and to express that willingness in some form – either by using a Radical Grieving worksheet, the 13 Steps to Radical Grieving Process, or a version of the Three Letter process. No matter which one we use, the process always requires that we go fully into our feelings. They work by connecting us to our Higher Self through our Spiritual Intelligence.

If there is some blame attached as well, perhaps even a need for revenge, then it will necessary to do a Radical Forgiveness worksheet in addition to the Radical Grieving worksheet. If there is some guilt to be released, then you may have to do a Radical Self-Forgiveness worksheet too. It is only in the use of these tools that the grief (once it is fully felt and acknowledged) will be transformed and anchored back in our body as a new way of looking at death. That's the fifth stage – Integration. But first, let's look at the basic assumptions underlying Radical Grieving that these tools will help us open up to.

Assumption #1. Our souls are immortal. When we incarnate, we take on a body in order to be able to experience separation emotionally. Our physical body is a temporary vehicle much prone to wearing out after a few score years. It helps us to do what we need to do to live life on the physical plane. When the time comes to revert to being solely in the World of Spirit, we drop the vehicle and return home. This means, then, that death is an illusion. It just looks like death to us because all we can see is a body.

This is what Jesus was trying to teach us in the Resurrection. There is no such thing as death. Not everyone does it quite like Jesus, of course, but millions of people have experienced a departed loved one appearing in a less-than-physical form (but unmistakably real nevertheless), and have had conversations with them. It is not at all uncommon. Others have received messages from people who have died, either directly from within themselves or via a medium, which could not have come from anyone else. In fact, I doubt there are many people alive today who do not believe that death is just a transition between one realm of existence and another. The evidence for it is irrefutable. Much as it tries to, science cannot prove anything to the contrary. Some of the theories that scientists come up with are infinitely more outrageous, stupid and improbable than the ones they try to refute. This is not surprising since science is, by definition, the study of the physical universe. It is not equipped to even begin looking at what is essentially mystical and non-physical. It simply doesn't have the tools.

Assumption #2. There is no such thing as an untimely death. The timing of our death is not a mistake. We choose the moment to go home, and it may have been decided before we incarnated. Who hasn't heard the saying, "When your number's up, that's it"? The implication there is clear. But we also have free will, so we can change it if we want to if, for instance, some opportunity arises that looks as if it would serve our soul's purpose to hang around for a little longer.

There's a story about a soul who decided he wanted to incarnate but only for a very short time. In a previous lifetime, he had known great opulence but had hoarded all his wealth. At the same time, he had deprived the people he ruled over of the basic necessities of life, and many had starved to death.

"Send me to be born in a place in the world where people are really starving," he said. "I want to experience that kind of deprivation as a way to balance my soul's energy. Set it up that I die of starvation after three years. That will be perfect for me."

So he went in, and after three years, his soul group stood around waiting for him to come back. He didn't come. One day, after all of 17 years had passed, he popped back up.

"Where have you been?" everyone asked. "You were only going to be a human for three years, and you have been away seventeen."

"I know," replied the soul. "I tried to live my mission, but those darn missionaries kept feeding me!"

Joking apart, our death is basically predetermined, and it happens when it is meant to happen. Who's to say that, in the grand scheme of things, dying at, say, age 25 is any worse or better than dying at 85, especially if there's a fair chance we come back again? Old age is not always very attractive anyway.

Assumption #3. The manner in which we die is also perfect. This is much more difficult for us to work with. People often say, "I am not afraid to die, but I am afraid that I might suffer a lot of pain in the process. It's how I might die that is the issue for me."

I think there is a lot more to it than that. Often the pain they talk about comes about through a deep need to resist death. Let's look more closely at this fear and see if the new paradigm answers the question of why people hang onto life at all costs, when on the face of it, to go home might be so nice. Let me take you back again to the conversation between Jack, the soul undergoing his pre-incarnation training, and Harley, the senior angel preparing him for it. Read how Harley explained the fear of death and why we have it.

"So what keeps people in the program?" I had to ask. "If life is as unpleasant as it sounds, why do people make such a strong point of doing it for as long as they can?"

"Simple," replied Harley. "The fear of death. The fear of ceasing to exist. That's what keeps them in the program. You have to hand it to the Ego, Jack. First it seduces you into believing that you are a separate entity, existing alone — separate from other human beings and from the source of infinite supply and security, God — and, to all intents and purposes, independent and self-reliant. Then it teaches you to fear death — which we up here know to be the way back home — to such a degree that you hang onto life at all costs, and never give up trying to keep death away. Fear of death, Jack. That's the motivation. Perfect, don't you think?"

"I guess it is," I agreed. "But is that the only purpose for making death fearful - to create a kind of prison without bars from which no one wants to escape?"

"There is more to it than that, Jack. The fear of death raises the bar for achieving a meaningful level of transcendence through the actual death process. If there was little fear, there would be little challenge to it. The journey of life is nothing more than a march towards death, and the purpose of life, my friend, is to face our worst fear and transcend it."

"How do we transcend it?" I enquired.

"By surrendering."

"Surrendering to what, though?"

"You'll find out, Jack. Until you know what it feels like to be in a human body facing death, you can't imagine how it is.

You will have spent the whole of your life thinking that you are sufficient unto yourself and in control of your destiny. As you slide towards death, you realize that you are powerless to control anything and that you are moving into the void, into nothingness, into non-existence. There's nothing more terrifying for human beings than the idea that they don't exist. And that's what death represents to them.

"We have set it up in precisely that way so that when they transcend their fear of death and go through the experience and discover that "not existing" means becoming once again ONE with God, their awareness of what that means will be magnified many hundreds of times. Can you see how that would raise the transcendence bar, Jack?"

"Yes, I think so," I replied thoughtfully. "It gives spiritual value to the whole experience. The higher the bar is set, the greater my growth through the process of transcendence. And in the moment that I find myself back home in this world, I will realize that my fear of death was in direct proportion to the bliss that I am feeling on this side."

*"That's right," said Harley. "Now you're starting to get it. **It is not death that is the doorway to the sublime; it's the fear of death.** The sublime arises in the realization that not only is death an illusion, but so is separation. Cool, isn't it? Up here, we have known that fact forever, of course. We know that separation is not the truth and just take it for granted that we souls exist in the same relationship to the Whole as a wave does in relation to the ocean. We think of Universal Intelligence as being a vast ocean of consciousness. Each one of us souls arises from that ocean and then, at the right and perfect moment, falls back into it to become one with it again.*

"For us then, death is nothing—just part of the song of existence. Since we know that we are existence itself, ceasing to exist is nothing to us, any more than it would be for a wave.

"But when you're human, you don't see it that way. Humans can't conceive of themselves just dying into the ocean of consciousness. They try to ensure their immortality," he continued, *"by imagining that they will come back again in a new lifetime as themselves, not realizing, of course, that once you have fallen back into the great sea of consciousness, into the ONENESS, you will never arise again as the same being - just as the wave that falls back into the ocean will never be that same wave again. In the same way that the ocean is constantly changing its form, God is continually recreating itself anew in every moment.*

"Transcending death in order to magnify our awareness of the LOVE vibration and ONENESS, is the great quest that each of us takes when we go down to the earth plane."

So, what Harley was saying here is that the fear of death keeps us in the game of separation and in the fear vibration; so in that sense, it is perfect. He also implies that the fear will dissipate fully only when we have died and gone home. However, since we are now waking up earlier to the fact that death is an illusion, we can at least partially expand into the Love vibration NOW by accepting death as the natural culmination of our mission on earth and the final healing of our separation. As a result of having stopped defining grief as being remorse over the death itself, as if it should not have happened, our pain and suffering is greatly reduced. Our grief then just becomes about our unbearable loss. It's not the death itself that's so tragic; it is that the person isn't here anymore. It would be no different if a person had gone to live on the other side of the world for good, never to be heard of again. That might

275

even be worse since we might construe it as a punishment or a rejection of us. Suicide apart, it's hard to think of someone's death as abandonment, even though it can feel like it sometimes.

Yet, having said all that, when it comes to the actual timing and manner of the person's death, we will have strong feelings, of course, as would any compassionate human being. Watching a person die in pain and agony is no moment for a spiritual bypass.

How unbearable would it be to have to imagine the scene in which one's own child is being murdered by a crazed rapist? How traumatizing was it to watch people throwing themselves out of the windows of the burning towers in New York City on that terrible day? Who did not wonder what it was like to die like that, and shudder? Who didn't want revenge on those who committed that crime? Who was able to walk through the gates of Auschwitz when it was liberated and not be sick to their stomach at what lay before them?

And of course, if someone dies at an early age, we will always wonder what kind of life he or she would have had if it had gone the full three score and ten? It does seem like a life wasted or cut short, and it brings sadness and tears to our eyes.

The AIDS epidemic cut short the lives of so many of our most gifted artists and performers who, we say, might have gone on for years gifting their extraordinary talents to humanity. Rudolph Nureyev, the Russian ballet dancer, the film star Rock Hudson and Freddie Mercury of the rock band Queen immediately come to my mind. What a terrible loss they and people like them were to humanity. But who knows what new talent they were they able to inspire from the other side? How do we know whether or not they might already be back in another body, contributing to humanity in some other way? We don't. But it's good to think that life goes on and that it all goes around in this way - nobody dying, nothing wasted, nothing lost.

So, not only will we, through the Radical Grieving process, reduce the intensity of our grief by draining it of all the erroneous assumptions about death itself, leaving only the raw pain of not having the person in our life any more, we might also help those going through the dying process in a very significant way. If we can be present with a person who is dying and able to see it not as a tragic event but as the person's moment of expansion into the love vibration, then we will be emitting the vibration of Love ourselves. We may even feel joy on their behalf because we know they are going home. If it is a loved one we are helping to transition, our own grief at the loss will come later.

Letting the Deceased Person Go
Another big benefit of Radical Grieving is that in taking on the idea that there was perfection in the death, exactly as it happened, it is less likely you will hold the person's soul back by grasping on. Seeing that your grief is very intense, long-lasting and full of anger and deep sadness, the departed soul might become unable to leave you and will remain stuck in the Astral plane, unable to fully go into the light. With Radical Grieving, this is much less likely.

Exercise:
In the same way that I say that all the tools we use to shift into the new paradigm help us to 'fake-it-till-we-make-it,' I suggest that you bring to mind again each one of the losses you listed in the first part of this chapter for transformation of your grief. Choose one to work on now and wait a few hours before working on the next one, if there is one. After you have run through, in your mind, the circumstances of the death and reminded yourself of his or her relationship with you and what he or she meant to you, read out loud, slowly and with awareness, each of the following statements.

1. In the wake of his/her death, I am allowing myself to feel how deeply I burn with grief over the loss. What a hole the loss has left in me! How my heart aches over the loss. I am focusing all my attention on the grief and allowing it to flow through my body. I am allowing the tears to come forth without restriction.

2. I claim my right to have such feelings and am willing to drop all judgments about my emotional state, knowing that no matter what I believe about death, it is essential that I feel my grief totally.

3. I am willing to see that a person's dying is an integral part of their life's journey, and the timing and circumstances of their death are all part of their divine plan and, at times, even a matter of choice. I am now willing to see that death is simply an illusion.

4. Knowing this now, I am willing to let go of all my judgments about this death and the circumstances in which it happened.

5. I am open to the idea that we all existed in spirit before we chose to take on a body as a way to purposely experience separation and that I will continue to exist, albeit in a state of oneness, after my body has ceased to be.

6. I am willing to be open to the idea that the death I am grieving was in a sense perfect and was meant to happen in that way.

7. I am open to the idea that in my willingness to accept the person's death as perfect, in the spiritual sense, I am making the person's transition easier, more peaceful and harmonious than it would otherwise be were I to continue seeing it as tragic or wrong.

8. Even though I know I am going to miss him/her, I am nevertheless beginning to feel more peaceful and accepting of the death itself, knowing that it was his/her choice to become free of the burden of having a physical body and to go home.

9. I am now finding myself letting go of the need to see the death as anything less than perfect and beginning now to feel a sense of peace both for myself and for him/her.

10. Death is neither a failure nor an unnatural occurrence. Coming to an acceptance of death as part of life itself brings a deeper meaning to our sense of loss and ultimately is the balm that heals our grief. As I now release him/her from any further need to be energetically attached to me, I am beginning to feel a little more peaceful now.

And so it is.

NOTE: *Once again, these statements are drawn from the audio process, '13 Steps to Radical Grieving,' which is to be found on the Radical Living Online Community membership site, www.colintipping.com/membership. If you have some grieving left to do, I would certainly recommend this process to help you complete it. Scan here to access it.*

Grief Over Something Other Than a Person or a Pet

When you lose something that was important to you, you will experience grief mixed in with a whole lot of other feelings: anger, frustration, fear, sadness, guilt and a whole range of feelings. Yes, it's different from losing a loved one; but no matter what it is that you have lost, you still need to feel the feelings and go through much the same process, albeit with a Radical Grieving perspective to soften the pain and speed it up.

It's an energy thing. A soldier who loses a limb in the war will need to grieve the loss of the leg or arm before he or she can go on and adjust to life without it. A person who loses the job he has been in for years and given his life to, will need to grieve it well before he will find another that will suit him. Without grieving the old one, he won't be able to attract the new job. Someone sentenced to several years in prison will need to grieve the loss of his or her freedom before he or she can function properly as a human being within that restricted environment. Someone who loses a relationship must grieve the loss of that relationship before he or she can successfully create a new one. Otherwise, he or she will take the old energy into the new one and lose that one too.

With the loss of a loved one through death, the shift that was asked of the griever was to open up the energy by reframing the death. The shift demanded of you, having lost something other than a person, is to reframe whatever has happened to you. In other words, once you have felt the feelings, gone through anger and depression and done a bit of bargaining in order to see a way forward, you then need to do the rest of the bargaining with Spirit by completing a reframe. By now, you should know exactly what I mean by that, so I won't bother to explain it. I will simply lead you into a Radical Grieving Process on whatever it is you might have lost and felt bad about losing. As before, complete the first two statements and then read all five out loud with awareness.

[We do offer an extended Online Radical Grieving Program for members and non-members which you might find very helpful if you are still in the grieving process. Scan the QR Code or go to www.colintipping.com/ online-programs.]

Exercise:
1. The thing that I lost that I valued highly and felt a lot of grief about losing it was: _____

2. I am entitled to feel bad about losing it and I own my feelings. I feel . . . _____

3. I recognize that there are no accidents in life and that, even though I will probably never understand why, there must be a reason for this to have happened. AGREE/DISAGREE

4. I am willing now to totally give up my attachment to the thing that is irretrievably gone from my life and trust that the Universe will support me no matter what. WILLING/UNWILLING

5. I am comfortable knowing that my Spiritual Intelligence knows what I need and that Spirit is the source of my supply at all times. AGREE/DISAGREE

The Abortion Issue
I cannot leave this chapter on grieving your losses without dealing with the subject of abortion. Many of those who have had an abortion, or been a party to that decision, carry a lot of pain around terminating a pregnancy and feel very guilty. Some experience it as a profound loss, especially if they were unable to conceive again and missed out on the chance to have children of their own.

Unfortunately, the issue of abortion has become extremely polarized. On one side, there are those who oppose it under any circumstances; and on the other side, there those who feel it is a personal choice. We don't hear much from people who might wish to find some sensible middle ground between the two extremes, although I am sure that most people would like to see a more nuanced position discussed. I do, however, think that in the way we conceive of it and how we treat people who are faced with the decision offers us a wonderful opportunity to expand into Love around this difficult philosophical issue.

Like most issues that become polarized to this extent, neither side can claim to know the answer to the basic spiritual questions that are at the core of the issue. Agreement is, therefore, impossible because while science tells us all about the intricacies of fertilization and cell division, it has nothing to say about the process by which a soul enters the body, and what happens to it if the pregnancy is terminated.

No one else knows the answer to that question either, and there is very little discussion about it. Most churches are dogmatic about it, but they are no better informed regarding the truth than anyone else. Both sides take positions on it based on assumptions which have no basis in fact but merely support their own prejudices.

This is exactly what I am about to do since I don't know either. All I can do, like everyone else, is come up with a story based on certain assumptions and inspired guesses about how we transition between the spiritual and physical realms through the processes of birth and death.

But first, let me say this. Abortion is an extremely important issue and is worthy of our deep consideration on ethical, social and spiritual grounds. There's no question in my mind about that. So I do not enter into this discussion lightly. I am also mindful of the fact that I am a man; and as such, I have no way of knowing what it is like to have the spiritual responsibility for giving life to a soul that requests to come through. Only a woman knows. Men need to honor this and have enough humility to admit that they are not privy to the same knowledge as women, and should be willing to defer to feminine wisdom when it comes to the process of giving life.

But that said, bearing in mind everything I have said before about the soul being immortal and having the ability to choose its parents and decide on its mission, I can easily imagine it might be disappointed if the woman it chooses to incarnate through says, "No, not right now." After all, that soul may have given a lot of thought to why that person was the ideal parent to experience life through. It may even have been an agreed soul contract between it and the soul of the mother.

But disappointment notwithstanding, I cannot imagine that the soul is mortally wounded if the mother says 'No,' even if it has already anchored itself in the form we call a fetus. If it was aborted, it would not be extinguished any more than a soul would who, as a baby, died a SIDS death, or the soul of a soldier killed in battle would be snuffed out. The soul cannot die. It simply goes back home to the spiritual realm, in all probability, no worse for wear but perhaps having experienced something instructive and valuable. And who is to say that the soul did not choose to have the abortion experience in order to balance the energy of having been a woman who aborted a fetus in a previous life.

This is not to say, however, that a woman and her partner who is, or should be, party to the decision should enter into this decision without a lot of careful and thoughtful consideration. There probably was a good reason why that soul requested passage into the human experience through her, and this has to be honored. One has to consider whether the reasons for saying 'No' are really good enough to support that decision given the opportunity being presented for both mother and future child. One has to consider all sides of the argument before making the decision.

But the prospective mother has a soul too, and her soul's wishes need to be honored as well. I think it is possible that the Spirit World, not really understanding how difficult life can be down here in the dense vibration of the physical realm, can sometimes put too much of a load on the shoulders of a soul who has taken on a body. I'm sure everything looks very easy from up there. I think they also understand that a soul who is in a human body is entitled to say "No" to whatever task he or she is being given at any one time. After all, it is a principle that we have free will and sometimes that freedom is exercised by saying "No" to a soul who is asking to incarnate through that soul's body.

I do think, however, that it is important that the woman says "No" as early as possible after discovering she is pregnant. Notwithstanding the fact that none of us know when the attachment actually happens, I can imagine that the more strongly the soul's energetic vibration has attached itself at the physical level, the more difficult it will be for it to detach and return home. And it need not necessarily be a total rejection. How often do we say to someone who wants something from us, "No, not now. Ask me again later." In other words, we might say to the soul, "Thank you for choosing me, but I'm just not ready for this now. Try again later when I am stronger and more prepared. I love you."

Again, as a man, I cannot say how any woman should go about making the decision, but I would respectfully suggest that it would be helpful to have a conversation with the soul that is knocking on the door. Talk to it and explain why you wish to refuse to be the conduit this time, and let it know that you are truly honored to be asked and that you love it dearly even though you are saying "No" on this occasion. Wish it well and tell it you hope to connect with it in another way if and when it incarnates. Then, be quiet and listen. Let the soul talk back to you. Maybe it will lovingly release you from the obligation and may tell you why you are so special and why it initially chose you.

Having had this kind of dialogue with you and feeling your love might be enough for the soul and satisfy its need to connect with you. Maybe, too, it will enable it to move on and find another woman to incarnate through. No harm done.

Afterword

Expanding into Love means empowering ourselves to live consciously, stay awake, live our purpose, keep our hearts open and remain connected in every moment to THE ALL THAT IS, no matter what is happening. At times, we shall fail. When we do, we must love ourselves for slipping back a little. We are still a work in progress.

As adolescents learning how to be fully awakened grown-ups, we still need to continue using the tools in a habitual way to help us expand ever deeper into Love. In particular, we need to use the whole range of Radical Living tools in our everyday lives in ways that systematically raise our vibration and expand our capacity to love: Radical Forgiveness, Radical Acceptance, Radical Awakening, and Radical Empowerment. Radical Transformation and Radical Manifestation,

These tools provide the bridge between the two paradigms, enabling us to consciously practice being in the new one while still operating in the other. Until mass consciousness makes that quantum leap and closes that consciousness gap, we must use that bridge.

The Radical Forgiveness tools will help us neutralize all past grievances and to deal peacefully with what's going on in the present moment, knowing that it is all perfect. Using the Radical

Acceptance tools will allow us to see the divinity in ourselves and all others. The Radical Transformation tools will help us transform outside events through our own shift in perception of what appears to be happening. Using Radical Manifestation tools, we can create our desired future in a conscious manner, deciding what to manifest, why we want it, what to do with it when it shows up and to what purpose. Through doing this, we identify our own life purpose, our goals and the values that align with our spiritual truth.

All this requires a high level of commitment to your spiritual growth. If you have come to this page having first read all the preceding pages, you must have that commitment. Otherwise, you would have put the book down a long time ago.

It also carries a responsibility to stay true to yourself, to know who you are and to own the power you possess to literally change the world. Your presence in the world at this special moment is extremely important. I hope you know that.

[To help you really connect with what Expanding into Love means, and to finish out the book, it seems right to finish with another 13 Step process. (Also available as a downloadable audio from the Radical Living Online Community membership website. www.colintipping.com/membership.]

13 Steps to Radical Empowerment

Step 1. As if from a vantage point outside of yourself, way above your head, take a moment to observe yourself as an awakened human being. See yourself as a spiritual being having a spiritual experience in a human body, having finally awakened to the reality of why you are here and for what purpose.

Step 2. Having completed the amount of separation you agreed to have in this lifetime, feel the joy that comes when you realize that

286

you are now free to live the remainder of your life committed to being the best human being that you can be, fully awake and aware of your divine self.

Now answer YES to the following questions

Step 3. As you look back at your life and see how you have created many opportunities to learn and grow, are you willing to give yourself credit for being willing to do this journey for your soul's growth and to fulfill your contract with others while on planet Earth?

Step 4. Even though you have awakened, are you willing to entertain the possibility that life will continue to arrange circumstances for you that will be challenging, will test your resolve to remain awake and on occasions tempt you to go back to Victimland?

Step 5. Will you be tolerant and forgiving of yourself if it should happen that you temporarily forget who you are and become unduly judgmental, critical or blaming towards others, knowing that this is what it still means to be imperfectly human — even if you are awake?

Step 6. Given that you might find yourself being upset with other people at times, will you, after feeling the feelings, be resolved to be quick to see the perfection in the situation and move swiftly to a state of peace and acceptance?

Step 7. Are you now willing to make Radical Forgiveness your default way of life by committing to do worksheets, listen to the 13 Steps or do the 4 step process, more or less on a daily basis, no matter how small the issue may seem, in order that you stay awake?

Step 8. Are you now able to see that, as an awake, spiritually aware human being, you have the power to manifest the life that you want and to make a difference in the world in line with your mission and purpose in ways not possible before?

Step 9. Are you, therefore, committed to developing your power to manifest that which contributes real and true value in the world for yourself and others through the use of the tools of Radical Manifestation, and by so doing raise the vibration of the planet?

Step 10. Are you now willing to accept the responsibility of being one of the few, perhaps soon to be many, who is able to hold and sustain a high vibration, even during the most difficult of circumstances that might seem catastrophic to the many others involved, and maintain a high intention to create an outcome that is for the highest and best for all involved?

Step 11. Are you willing to accept the fact that if you continue to use the Radical Forgiveness and Radical Manifestation technology in a sustained way, you will reach a point where you will be vibrating at high enough frequency to shift the consciousness of the human race?

Step 12. As you feel your connectedness with everyone and everything in the Universe, are you able to fully accept your capacity, as one among many who vibrate at the same frequency, to create world peace and are you willing to hold that intention now?

Step 13. Finally, are you willing to let go of any attachment to being awake, to making a difference, to creating world peace or manifesting anything of any consequence, knowing that in surrendering to what is - as is, you are trusting the Universe to take care of whatever needs to happen?

AND SO IT IS!

APPENDIX I

Additional Resources

The following are available from the FREE section of the Radical Living Online Community membership site: Scan this QR Code to access the Free area or go to *www.colintipping.com/membership*

1. WORKSHEETS TO DOWNLOAD (AS PDF)
- The Radical Forgiveness Worksheet
- The Radical Manifestation Worksheet
- The Money Consciousness Worksheet
- The Radical Acceptance of Another Worksheet
- The PowerShift Group (Instructions)
- The Radical Forgiveness Support Group (Instructions)

[Note: Online versions of these tools that offer a lot more interactivity and 'on-screen' participation by the user are available to members of the Radical Living Online Community. See Appendix II.]

2. FREE READS
- Jill's Story
- A Wake for the Inner Child
- Radical Forgiveness: A Complementary Cancer Treatment
- Epilogue 9/11
- Body Syndromes

3. ONLINE PROGRAMS (PAID)
- The Self-Forgiveness/Self-Acceptance Program
- The Radical Manifestation Program
- 21-Day Program for Forgiving Parents
- 21-Day Program for Forgiving Siblings
- 21-Day Program for Forgiving Partner/s
- 21-Day Program for Forgiving Your Kids
- A 21-Day Program for Forgiving Your Co-Workers
- The Online X4 Radical Money Program
- Colin Tipping's Radical Weight Loss Program

[To discover more about these online programs and how they can help you, go to www.colintipping.com/online-programs or scan the QR Code.]

4. COACHES
There may come a time when you simply need someone you can talk with about the issues you are dealing with. Our Radical Living Coaches and Radical Forgiveness Therapy Practitioners are there to help and are listed on the website. For the list, go to www.colintipping.com/coaching or scan the code.

5. OTHER RESOURCES
For many more resources including other books by Colin Tipping, CDs, DVDs, game and other products, scan the QR Code or visit the e-Store: www.colintipping.com/e-Store.

APPENDIX II

The Radical Living Online Community

(A Membership Site)

The Radical Living Online Community is a virtual community dedicated to supporting people who are committed to their spiritual growth, are determined to stay awake and have a high intention to develop the Radical Living lifestyle.

As you have discovered at several points in this book, there are many resources, in addition to the free ones and paid programs listed in Appendix I, that are exclusive to members. They are all mobile compatible and able to be accessed on Macs and PCs as well as mobile devices. These are:

a) Special Online Interactive Tools
1. The Radical Forgiveness Online Worksheet Program
2. The Radical Self-Forgiveness Online Worksheet Program
3. The Radical Transformation Online Worksheet Program
4. The Radical Manifestation Online Worksheet Program
5. The Radical Relationship Assessment Worksheet Program
6. The Balancing Humenergy Online Worksheet for Business.
7. The Emerge-N-See 4-Step Process
8. Radical New Career Manifestation Program
9. Radical Wealth Retrieval Program
10. Relationship Assessment Questionnaire
11. Radical Reconciliation Worksheet
11. Manifesting a New Relationship Worksheet
12. The 'Boundaries' Worksheet

b) The Online Audio 13-Steps Processes (mp3)
The 13 Steps to Radical Forgiveness Process
The 13 Steps to Radical Self Forgiveness Process
The 13 Steps to Radical Transformation Process Audio
The 13 Steps to Radical Awakening Process Audio
The 13 Steps to Radical Grieving Process Audio
The 13 Steps to Creating Funding for a Project Audio
The 13 Steps to Radical Weight Loss Audio
The 13 Steps to Creating a Job Audio
The 13 Steps to Radical Empowerment Audio.

c) Online Events
As a member you will be able to participate in regular webinars
and Q&A sessions as well as engage in online discussion/study
groups focused on readings from my books, interviews with
interesting people and many other engaging group activities.

d) Mutual Support
Being a member means being part of a high vibration online
community. That means being able to share stories, give and
receive support, post comments and ask questions. We need
each other!

*[To discover more about the benefits of being a
member of the Radical Living Online Community,
www.colintipping.com/membership or scan
the QR Code.]*

About the Author

Born in England in 1941, Colin was raised during the war in early post-war Britain by working-class parents. He has an elder brother and a younger sister. By his own account his parents were good people, loving and hardworking and he considers himself blessed in having had a stable and enjoyable childhood in spite of the social hardships of the time.

His degree is in Education and he lectured at London University and Middlesex University from 1973 - 1983. He immigrated to America in 1984 and shortly thereafter became certified as a clinical hypnotherapist. In 1992, he and his wife JoAnn, whom he met in Atlanta and married in 1990, created a series of healing retreats in the north Georgia mountains for people challenged with cancer. In recognizing that lack of forgiveness was a big part of the causation, they set about refining a new form of forgiveness that the people would be able to do with ease and grace. This was the birth of Radical Forgiveness. The method by which it was applied with great success was called The Tipping Method.

In 1997 he wrote the first edition of the book, *Radical Forgiveness* and has since authored many other books in addition to producing a series of practical online healing programs. The main characteristic of his work is a practical spirituality that is simple, honest, straight-forward and unpretentious. While he never claims to know the truth, and is happy to live in the mystery of the question, he loves to muse and create 'stories' that, at least, make sense to our limited minds and resonate with our inner knowingness.

293

He has a knack for making spiritual issues simple and practical. He believes that spirituality is useless if it cannot be used in a practical way in our everyday life. His books all have a practical side to them as do his workshops.

Colin is leading the way in preparing the population for the imminent Global Awakening. For many years Colin's mission statement has been: *"To Raise the Consciousness of the Planet Through Radical Forgiveness and To Create a World of Forgiveness by 2012."* He has spent the last 12 years perfecting the tools that we all can use to make this happen. They raise our vibration and help us maintain our inner peace as we go through this transitional period.

Colin Tipping now takes a form of the Tipping Method into corporations and other organizations as a way to resolve and prevent conflict, raise morale and increase productivity. His book, *Spiritual Intelligence At Work,* explains the rationale for this system.

Training Others to Spread the Word
In 2000 Colin and JoAnn Tipping founded the Institute for Radical Forgiveness Therapy and Coaching, Inc., and has since trained many coaches and practitioners in the U.S. and many countries overseas,

> *[If you are interested in becoming a Radical Living Coach or a Radical Forgiveness Therapy Practitioner, scan this QR code to see the range of certification courses offered at www. theInstituteforRadicalForgiveness.com. Not all require previous qualifications.]*

TO CONTACT:
E-mail at support@radicalforgiveness.com